180 Think-Aloud Math Word Problems

by Denise Nessel and Ford Newbold

S C H O L A S T I C
PROFESSIONALBOOKS

NEW YORK • TORONTO • LONDON • AUCKLAND • SYDNEY
MEXICO CITY • NEW DELHI • HONG KONG • BUENOS AIRES

Cover design by Maria Lilja
Cover and interior illustrations by Michael Moran
Interior design by Solutions by Design, Inc.

ISBN: 0-439-40074-0

6 7 8 9 10   40   09 08 07 06

Contents

Think-Aloud Word Problems

ADDITION AND SUBTRACTION

MULTIPLICATION AND DIVISION

MONEY

MEASUREMENT

FRACTIONS AND PERCENTS

RATES, AVERAGES, AND LOGICAL REASONING

Introduction

180 Think-Aloud Math Word Problems offers students a simple yet powerful approach to understanding and solving word problems. Each of the problems in this book is presented in three parts—the initial premise, additional information, and the question to answer—so kids can stop, read, and make predictions at each step. Introduce the problems as group lessons or independent activities—one for each day of the school year! This unique "read-and-think" approach helps kids learn effective strategies for tackling word problems while building skills in multiplication, division, time, money, fractions, and more. It's also a great way to prepare kids for standardized tests.

We've used the read-and-think strategy with great success in classrooms around the country. Start by presenting the first part of a problem—the initial premise—on an overhead projector or on the chalkboard. Then ask kids to discuss the following questions:

* ❋ Based on the information we have so far, what do you think the question might be? What do you think we are going to have to figure out?

* ❋ Why do you think so?

* ❋ Do we have all the information we need to answer this question? If not, what other information do we need?

* ❋ What operations do you think we'll have to perform?

Next, reveal the second part of the problem. Ask kids to discuss the above questions again and revise their predictions based on the new information. Finally, reveal the question and have students solve the problem.

Challenging students to predict the question makes them more curious about what the question will be. When students make predictions, they pay closer attention to details and nuances of meaning, which sharpens their thinking and improves their comprehension. For years, experts have advocated the practice of making predictions while reading (Stauffer, 1969; Britton, 1970; Weaver, 1988). The latest research supports prediction-making as an effective learning strategy in any subject area (Nystrand, 1997; Marzano, 2001).

The read-and-think approach encourages kids to be more attentive, enthusiastic, and involved in the problem-solving process. By working through each problem in steps, they will read more carefully and gain a deeper understanding of what they are being asked to do. By the time the question is finally revealed, students will be ready to answer it with greater interest than if they had been presented with a traditional word problem. And because the process helps build a better understanding of the problem, they are more likely to answer the question correctly. Using this approach, students build problem-solving skills—as well as confidence in their ability to tackle word problems—that will serve them well in school, on standardized tests, and in real-life situations.

How to Use This Book

There are 180 problems in this book—one for each day of the school year. The problems are organized into 30 sets, with six problems in each. Refer to the table of contents to find the topic that is covered in each set, such as fractions, money, and measurement. At the end of the book, you'll find an answer key that shows you step by step how to solve the problems. Some problems have an alternate question in parentheses that can be used instead of or in addition to the original question. Answers for alternate questions are also provided in the answer key. In addition, the appendix on pages 79–80 shows how you might work through two different problems using the read-and-think strategy. You may want to use these as models to help students become more effective with this approach.

Using the Read-and-Think Approach

Introduce the read-and-think approach by explaining and modeling the process for students. Start with a short, simple problem. You might present the problem on an overhead transparency or write it on a sheet of chart paper. Cover the problem with another sheet of paper so that you can reveal one part at a time. Or, write each part of the problem on a strip of transparency film or paper and display one strip at a time.

Have students work with partners or in small groups. Display the first part of the problem and pose the following questions:

* Based on the information we have so far, what do you think the question might be? What do you think we are going to have to figure out?

* Why do you think so?

* Do we have all the information we need to answer this question? If not, what other information do we need?

* What operations do you think we'll have to perform?

Have students discuss these questions with their partner or group and then share their ideas with the whole class. Encourage students to generate at least two possible questions using the information they know so far. Next, reveal the second part of the problem. Again, have kids discuss the above questions with their partner or in small groups. Explain that they may have to revise their predictions based on the new information. Then invite the partners or groups to share their ideas with the class. Finally, reveal the question and have students answer it, either individually or in small groups.

Walking Through a Sample Problem

Here's an example of how to use the read-and-think approach with a sample problem.

Mike and David are on the same baseball team, the Rockets. Their team played in a game on Friday.

From the information given in the first part of the problem, there are many questions that could work as the final question. Here are some possibilities:

* ❋ By how much did the Rockets win (or lose) the game?
* ❋ What were Mike's and David's batting averages for this game?
* ❋ How many more hits did David get than Mike?
* ❋ How did this game affect the Rockets' standing in their league?
* ❋ How many miles per hour did they average on their way to the game?
* ❋ What is the average age of the players on the Rockets?
* ❋ How much will the Rockets' new uniforms cost all together?

Demonstrate for students how to use the limited information in the first part of the problem to generate possible questions. Here's an example of what you might say to model effective thinking at each stopping point:

This is all I know so far, so I'm not sure what the question will be. Let me see if I can think of some possibilities. The question might have to do with how many hits or runs Mike and Dave got, or perhaps how many balls they caught, or maybe how often they were up to bat. Any of those could be determined for each boy separately or as totals for the two together. Or maybe the question will ask us to compare some aspect of their performance with the performance of other players. If I have to figure out how many hits or runs they got all together, or how many times they were up to bat, I might have to add. But if I have to compare their performance with the performance of other players, I might have to subtract. There might be other operations I'd have to do, too. I need more information before I can decide.

Mike got four hits in the game on Friday; David got three.

This makes me think I'll be asked how many hits they got altogether. Or maybe the question will ask how many more hits Mike got than Dave. If it's the first, I'll have to add. If it's the second, I'll have to subtract.

How many hits did they get in all?

Now I know that I have to add Mike's and Dave's hits together to get the answer. That means adding 4 and 3.

Leading the Discussion

Thinking of possible questions helps students apply math concepts in different ways and become more flexible in their thinking. Explain to students that the purpose of this exercise is not to predict the actual question, but rather to generate any reasonable question based on the information given. Students often suggest questions that are as interesting and challenging to solve as the one provided.

Throughout this process, encourage students to explore their ideas carefully and thoroughly. Guide them to explain their reasoning, consider alternative hypotheses, listen to one another, and build upon one another's ideas. The following illustrates a discussion based on the first part of a sample word problem.

Your class is planning a holiday party, and your teacher asks you to help with the plans. There are 25 students in the class, plus the teacher and a parent volunteer. Everyone wants punch.

Teacher: What do you think the question might be?

Student A: How much punch will they have to buy?

Teacher: Why does that seem likely?

Student A: It says, "help with the plans," and planning for a party usually means you have to figure out how much stuff to get.

Student B: Yes, and it says everyone wants punch, so the question is probably going to be about punch.

Teacher: What operations would you have to use if you have to figure out how much to buy?

Student C: Does punch come in gallons?

Student D: I think so, or maybe quarts. We'd have to figure out how many cups in a gallon or a quart and see if that would be enough for 25 people. We'd have to divide, I think.

Student E: There are 27 people if you count the teacher and the parent volunteer. And people might have more than one cup of punch.

Student A: How many cups are there in a gallon?

Teacher: We'd have to figure that out. Any other ideas about what the question might be?

Student B: We might have to figure out how much the punch will cost. We'd figure out how much they need, and then we'd have to multiply the cost of one gallon by the number of gallons. Or quarts, or whatever the size is.

180 Think-Aloud Math Word Problems Scholastic Professional Books

Teacher: Any other ideas?

Student C: We might have to figure out how many glasses and napkins they'll need. Or we might need to find out how much ice they'll need.

Teacher: Why does that seem likely?

Student C: It says they all like punch, so they'll need cups and napkins in case they spill.

Teacher: What operations would you need to use?

Student D: You might have to figure out how many cups and napkins there are in a package and see if that's enough. If they need more than one package, then you'd have to multiply the cost of one package by the number of packages they need.

Teacher: Good thinking, everyone! Let's read the next part of the problem. Then we can decide if we're going to keep any of those ideas or if we'd like to make different predictions.

Tips

* Present short, easy problems until students are comfortable with the process and understand how to predict questions.

* Each day, choose a problem from a different set. The variety will help students learn to think flexibly when solving problems.

* Change the details in the problems to make them more relevant to students. For instance, use students' names or topics that tie into their own experiences. You might also make up your own problems, using the ones in this book as models.

* Have students work together before they work independently. Working in pairs or small groups helps students understand the read-and-think process more quickly. When students work together, they are able to build upon one another's ideas, notice more details, generate more questions, and solve problems more effectively.

* Encourage students to take notes and solve the problems in their own read-and-think notebooks. At each stopping point, have them write their thoughts and predictions.

* Have students take turns guiding the class through the read-and-think process.

* Have students use the read-and-think approach to solve problems in their math textbook or supplementary materials.

Follow-Up Activities

Once students have become familiar with this approach, have them try one or more of these extensions to improve their problem-solving skills.

* ✳ After students solve a problem, have them compare their answers and approaches. Such analysis is especially useful for complicated problems that can be solved in more than one way. As students discuss and justify their reasoning, they will refine their skills and learn useful strategies from one another.

* ✳ Have students write read-and-think problems for their classmates to solve. Challenge students to follow the three-part format of the problems in this book. As they write the problems, have them create an answer key that shows, step by step, how to solve the problems. Encourage them to include any explanatory notes or drawings that might be helpful in illustrating the solutions. Students can use the same first part of a problem in the book and then change the second and third parts. Here are two examples of problems that could be created based on the baseball problem on page 7.

Mike and David are on the same team, the Rockets. Their team played in a game on Friday.
Mike is 11 years old, and David is 12. Of the other seven players on the team, three are
Mike's age, three are David's age, and one is 10.
What is the average age of the players on the team?

Mike and David are on the same team, the Rockets. Their team played in a game on Friday.
In one game, Mike got 4 hits and David got 5 hits. In another game, Mike got 3 hits and
David got 6 hits.
In those two games, which boy got more hits? How many more?

Have students make up read-and-think problems based on data found in books, magazines, or online sources. For instance, a bar graph in a newspaper showed the percentage of people living in rural areas in the United States in each decade from 1950 through the year 2000. Students could use this graph to generate problems such as:

In 1950, 70% of the U.S. population lived in a rural area.
In 1990, 18% fewer people were living in rural areas.
What percent of the population lived in a rural area in 1990?

Have students take their notebook entries one step further by explaining how they solved problems. Ask them to include what steps they took and their reasoning behind such steps. Students can add sketches as necessary. They might also reflect on the predictions that other students made. Which questions were plausible with the information given? Which ones were not, and why?

References

Britton, James. *Language and Learning* (Penguin, 1970).

Marzano, Robert J., Debra J. Pickering, and Jane E. Pollock. *Classroom Instruction That Works* (Association for Supervision and Curriculum Development, 2001).

Nystrand, Martin, with Adam Gamoran, Robert Kachur, and Catherine Prendergast. *Opening Dialogue* (Teachers College Press, 1997).

Stauffer, Russell. *Teaching Reading as a Thinking Process* (Harper & Row, 1969).

Weaver, Constance. *Reading Process and Practice* (Heinemann Educational Books, 1988).

ADDITION AND SUBTRACTION: SET 1

Finding Totals

1 Joe likes to collect and trade watches. On Friday, he had 23 watches in his collection.

On Saturday, he went to a flea market and bought 4 more watches for $2.00 each. On Sunday, he went to 3 garage sales and bought 2 watches at each sale for $1.00 each.

How many watches did Joe have on Sunday after his last purchase?

ALTERNATE QUESTION: *How much did the new watches cost him all together?*

2 Rosa's father gave her 42 stamps. Her goal is to have a collection of 100 stamps.

She bought 12 stamps at a shop and ordered 9 stamps from a magazine. Then she bought a special set of 14 stamps from the post office.

How many does she still need to reach her goal?

3 Shawn has 440 basketball cards so far. By the end of the month, he wants to own a total of 500.

The cards come in packs of 5. The first week of the month, he bought 4 packs of cards. The second week, he bought 3 packs. He bought 2 packs during the third week and 2 packs during the fourth week.

Did he reach his goal of 500 cards?

180 Think-Aloud Math Word Problems Scholastic Professional Books

4 Bridget Baxter's mother has 28 refrigerator magnets. The Baxters decide to give Mrs. Baxter more magnets for her birthday.

Bridget gives her mother 2 magnets. Her brother gives their mother 4 magnets. Bridget's 2 sisters give their mother 3 magnets each, and Mr. Baxter gives his wife a set of 5.

After receiving her gifts, how many magnets does Mrs. Baxter have all together?

ALTERNATE QUESTION: *How many magnets did the family give Mrs. Baxter all together?*

5 Ernie loves waffles. On Monday he ate 3 waffles. On Tuesday, he ate 6 waffles.

For the next 3 days, he ate 2 waffles a day. On Saturday and Sunday, he ate 4 waffles each day.

How many waffles did Ernie eat that week all together?

6 Boris and Eddie played their favorite video game 2 hours a day for 4 days in a row.

On Monday, Boris earned 500 points and Eddie earned 450. On Tuesday, Boris earned 350 points and Eddie earned 520. On Wednesday, Boris earned 200 points and Eddie earned 180. On Thursday, Boris earned 600 points and Eddie earned 570.

Who had the most points at the end of the four days?

Using Inference to Find Totals

1 One week Toni found pennies on the sidewalk every day on the way to school. On Monday, she found 2 pennies. On Tuesday, she found 3 more than she found on Monday.

On Wednesday, Toni found 2 more than she found on Tuesday. On Thursday, she found 2 more than she found on Wednesday. On Friday, she found the same number of pennies that she found on Monday.

How much money did she find all together?

2 Mr. Wong's class decided to tally the taxis, buses, and trucks they could see from the classroom window between 9 A.M. and 9:30 A.M. on two days. They formed 3 groups to do the counting.

On Monday, Group 1 counted 24 taxis, Group 2 counted 7 buses, and Group 3 counted 31 trucks. On Tuesday, Group 1 counted 2 more taxis than they counted on Monday. Group 2 counted 1 fewer bus than on Monday, and Group 3 counted 3 more trucks than on Monday.

How many of each kind of vehicle did the students count all together?

ALTERNATE QUESTION: *How many vehicles did they count all together?*

3 Alexa, Barker, and Crystal entered a charity walkathon. Their sponsors agreed to give $1.00 for each mile they walked.

Alexa had 10 sponsors, and she walked 4 miles. Barker had 12 sponsors, and he walked the same distance as Alexa. Crystal had 20 sponsors, and she walked 1 more mile than Alexa.

How much money did the 3 walkers raise all together?

4 During a rainy spell, a class measured the amount of rainfall each day for 5 days.

On Monday, they measured 1 inch of rain. On Tuesday, they measured twice as much as on Monday. On Wednesday, they measured 3 inches. On Thursday, they measured the same amount as on Tuesday. On Friday, they measured 1 inch.

How much did it rain all together from Monday through Friday?

5 Daisy and Eduardo manage the school store, which is open on Monday, Wednesday, and Friday. They sell pencils for 10 cents each and erasers for 25 cents each. One week they had especially good sales.

On Monday, they sold 20 pencils and 6 erasers. On Wednesday, they sold half as many pencils and twice as many erasers as on Monday. On Friday, they sold twice as many pencils as on Monday and twice as many erasers as on Wednesday.

How many pencils did they sell all together, and how many erasers?

ALTERNATE QUESTION: *How much money did they collect that week from sales of pencils and erasers?*

6 The cafeteria at Adams School sells apple crunch bars for 50 cents. The cashier kept track of how many bars they sold each week for a month.

The first week, they sold 98 bars. The second week, they sold 100 more than they sold the first week. The third week, they sold half as many as they did the second week. The fourth week, they sold 107 bars.

How many bars were sold in total over the 4 weeks?

ALTERNATE QUESTION: *What was the total amount of money taken in from the sale of the bars in 4 weeks?*

ADDITION AND SUBTRACTION: SET 3

Figuring Totals After Exchanges

1 Barry and Brian like to play marbles. One Saturday morning, Barry had 56 marbles and Brian had 47 marbles.

They played for 3 hours on Saturday afternoon. Barry won 9 marbles from Brian and Brian won 12 marbles from Barry.

How many marbles did each boy have in the end?

2 Christine and Carmen often borrowed money from each other. At the beginning of the week, Christine had $8.69 and Carmen had $7.36.

On Monday, Carmen lent Christine $1.25 for lunch and spent $1.40 for her own lunch. The next day, Christine lent Carmen $1.40 for lunch and spent $1.80 for her own lunch.

How much did each girl have on Wednesday before they paid each other back?

3 Carlos and Frank practice tennis together at the public courts. One Saturday, they took 40 tennis balls with them.

They couldn't find 8 tennis balls they hit into the bushes and 5 that landed in the creek. Squirrels ran off with 3 more. They found 4 tennis balls on their court and kept those.

How many tennis balls did they have at the end of the day?

ALTERNATE QUESTION: *How many did they lose all together?*

180 Think-Aloud Math Word Problems Scholastic Professional Books

4 Angelica had 63 charms in her collection and Brittany had 49 in hers when they decided to trade charms.

Angelica gave Brittany 13 charms, and Brittany gave Angelica 7 charms.

How many did each girl have after the trade?

ALTERNATE QUESTION: *Which girl had more charms at the end?*

5 Gamel put $3.50 in change in his pocket and set off to buy a goldfish. When he got to the store, he discovered that some of his money had fallen through a hole in his pocket. He had only $2.39.

When he went back to look for his money, he found a one-dollar bill, 3 pennies, and 1 dime.

How much did he have after finding the money?

ALTERNATE QUESTION: *How much did he lose on the way to the store?*

6 Ms. Penny's class was responsible for bringing balloons to the school festival. Each of the 28 students brought in 1 package of 5 balloons, and the class went outside to blow them up.

As they were inflating the balloons, 24 popped and 11 blew away. Ms. Penny found 2 more packages of 5 balloons in her desk, and the students inflated those without losing a single one.

How many inflated balloons did the class have all together at the end?

Finding an Age

1   Diana's grandmother was born in 1939. She was 30 years old when Diana's mother was born.

Diana's mother was born in 1969, and Diana was born in 1993.

How old was Diana's grandmother when Diana was born?

2   Flora's father bought a 1957 Chevy for $4,000 in 1985 when Flora was 10 years old.

He kept the car for 12 years, and then he sold it for $6,000.

How old was the car when he sold it?

3   Timmy got a 2-month-old puppy for his ninth birthday in June. The puppy weighed 15 pounds, and Timmy named him Bear.

Timmy expects to keep Bear until he graduates from high school at the age of 18.

How old will Bear be when Timmy graduates from high school?

4 Sumi moved to the United States with her parents in 1994, when she was 2 years old. The family moved to Iowa 2 years later.

After living in Iowa for 3 years, the family moved to Virginia. In the year 2000, they moved to Florida.

How old was Sumi when her family moved to Florida?

5 Tyrone's grandfather was born in January 1942. Tyrone's father was born in January 1968.

Tyrone was born in January 1995.

How old were Tyrone's grandfather and father when Tyrone was born?

6 Skip's grandfather, who was born in 1936, had a special guitar made for himself in 1960. He gave the guitar to Skip's father for his eighteenth birthday in 1984.

Skip's father gave the guitar to Skip for his fourteenth birthday in 2003.

How old was the guitar when Skip received it?

ALTERNATE QUESTION: *How old was Skip's grandfather when Skip received his special guitar?*

Finding the Year of Birth

1 Abraham Lincoln, the sixteenth president of the United States, was born on February 12.

If Lincoln were still alive in the year 2000, he would have celebrated his 191st birthday on February 12 of that year.

In what year was Lincoln born?

2 In 2001, Rayna created a family tree. She wrote 1938 as the year of her grandmother's birth and 1906 as the year of her great-grandmother's birth.

Rayna's mother looked at the tree and said, "Oops! You've got the wrong year of birth for your great-grandmother. She was 37 years old when my mother was born, not 32."

In what year was Rayna's great-grandmother born?

3 Thomas Jefferson wrote the first draft of the Declaration of Independence in Philadelphia in 1776 and became president of the United States 25 years later.

Jefferson was 57 years old when ran for president in 1800. He and Aaron Burr received the same number of votes, so Congress had to decide who would be president. In February of 1801, after 36 ballots, Jefferson won and took office soon after.

In what year was Thomas Jefferson born?

4 In 2002, Monica found a postcard that her grandfather had sent to her grandmother when they were young. The postcard was mailed on July 3, 1954. They were married 4 years later.

Monica's grandfather was 18 years old when he sent the card.

In what year was Monica's grandfather born?

5 Booker T. Washington was born in Virginia and later moved to Tuskegee, Alabama.

In 1881, Booker T. Washington became principal of Tuskegee Institute. He was 25 years old.

In what year was Booker T. Washington born?

6 When the United States declared its independence in 1776, the capital was in Philadelphia. George Washington, who became president in 1789 at the age of 57, decided that the new country should have a new capital.

Washington chose the site for the new capital in 1791. Nine years later, everything was ready and the federal government moved to the new capital, Washington, D.C.

In what year did Washington, D.C., become the official capital of the United States?

Multiplying and Adding Products

1 Wendy's cat Sugar had 6 kittens. All the kittens were female.

Each of Sugar's kittens had kittens, too. Each had 6 females and 2 males.

How many "grandchildren" did Sugar have all together?

2 Washington School was having a fund-raiser, and the third-grade classes decided to make cookies and sell them.

Each of the 4 third-grade classes made 3 dozen cookies every school day for a week.

How many cookies did the third-graders make all together?

3 Mr. Lee's class of 24 students held a 4-week reading contest. They set a class goal of reading 250 books during that time.

During the first 2 weeks, half the class read 2 books each per week, and the other half read 3 books each per week. During the last 2 weeks, half the class read 3 books each per week, and the other half read 4 books each per week.

Did the class reach its goal?

4 Mrs. Otto gave her 25 students a challenge. For the next 3 weeks, each student who earned 90% or better on the weekly math quiz would receive 5 points. If the class as a whole earned 300 points in 3 weeks, she would treat them all to pizza.

The first week, 18 students scored 90% or better. The second week, 20 students scored 90% or better, and the third week, all the students scored over 90%.

Did the class get its pizza?

5 At Jackson School in Minnesota, there are 52 students in kindergarten, 70 in first grade, 74 in second grade, and 82 in third grade. During the winter, the children wear warm clothing to school.

On very cold days, all the children wear hats and boots, and they wear either mittens or gloves.

If all the children wear mittens on the same day, how many mittens are worn all together?

6 Takisha's mother got a new cell phone with a plan that allows 400 minutes of calls each month for $15.95. The plan charges extra if she uses more than 400 minutes. She asked Takisha to keep track of the minutes she uses.

In the first week, she used 15 minutes each day for 5 days, and in the second week she used 25 minutes a day for 4 days. In the third week she used 32 minutes each day for 4 days, and in the fourth week, she used 20 minutes a day for 4 days.

Did Takisha's mother stay within the 400-minute limit?

Dividing Food

1 Kevin invited 4 friends to his house for a party and ordered pizza for everyone.

Kevin ordered 4 pizzas. Each was cut into 8 slices.

If each person eats 4 slices of pizza, how many slices will be left over?

2 Jenna goes camping with 3 friends. She brings 24 granola bars because she and her friends all like them.

Each camper eats 2 granola bars a day.

How long will the bars last?

3 Omar goes to the movies with Sean and Maurice. Each boy buys a bag of candy and agrees to share with the others.

Omar's bag has 24 pieces of candy. Sean's bag has 15 pieces. Maurice's bag has 18 pieces.

If they divide the candy equally, how many pieces will each boy get?

ALTERNATE QUESTION: *If each bag of candy cost $2.50, how much did the boys pay all together?*

4 Mr. Murray brought 2 cakes for the class. Each cake was cut into 24 pieces.

Mr. Murray asked the class to figure out how many pieces each student could have if they were to share them equally.

There are 20 students in the class. How many pieces did each one get?

ALTERNATE QUESTION: *How many students could have another piece?*

5 When Ravi brought 3 friends to his house after school, his mother gave them a box of pretzels and a box of crackers. She told them to share the snacks equally among themselves and to give her any that were left over.

The boys opened the boxes and found a total of 26 pretzels and 35 crackers.

How many pretzels and crackers did the boys give to Ravi's mother?

6 Carlene and Danielle each bought one package of gum at the supermarket. Each package had 5 pieces.

While they waited for the bus, Suki joined them, and they each gave her one piece of gum. Then Ana joined them, and Carlene and Danielle each gave Ana one piece of gum.

How many pieces of gum did each girl have?

MULTIPLICATION AND DIVISION: SET 8

Determining Shares of Total Costs

1 The 3 fifth-grade classes at Kimball School want to go to a baseball game.

It will cost $675 for the students in all 3 classes to go. Each class has the same number of students.

How much money does each class have to raise so that everyone can make the trip?

2 The fifth-grade classes at Franklin School are going to a basketball game. The group will hire buses to take them to the game. There are 25 students in one class, 22 in the second class, and 28 in the third class.

There will be 3 teachers and 7 parents going as chaperones. The only buses available hold 17 passengers, and each one costs $34 for a round trip.

How many buses are needed?

ALTERNATE QUESTION: *How much does each person have to pay for the bus transportation?*

3 Mr. Mayer is retiring after 30 years of teaching. His 28 students want to buy him a new pair of binoculars for a retirement present.

The gift committee finds a pair of binoculars for $50.00 and a card for $1.50. With tax, the total comes to $55.62.

If every student chips in $2.00, will they have enough to pay for the present and the card?

4 Mrs. Khan and her fourth-grade class want to help wild animals by buying a membership to the Wild Animal Society. A one-year group membership costs $45.00.

There are 29 students in Mrs. Khan's class.

How much does each person have to contribute so that the group will have enough for a membership?

5 Luis's 4 best friends decide to take Luis to the movies on his birthday. Each friend will pay for himself and for $\frac{1}{4}$ of Luis's costs.

Matinee tickets cost $5.00. The boys also want to buy popcorn and drinks for everyone. Popcorn costs $3.00 a box and a large soft drink costs $2.00.

How much will each friend have to spend in all to buy tickets and treats for himself and Luis?

6 Rebecca and her 3 friends all want the same new video game, which costs $54.95, not including tax. None of the girls can afford to buy the game on her own.

They decide to buy the game together and share it.

If the tax on the game is $4.45, how much does each girl have to chip in?

Determining If There Is Enough for Everyone

1 A ream of paper has 500 sheets in it.

Each student in Mrs. Andersen's class needs 20 sheets for a class project.

If there are 26 students in the class, will one ream of paper be enough?

2 There are 8 students on the Math Whiz team, and their coach decides to give each one 4 pencils with "Math Whiz" printed in gold.

The pencils come in packages of 12.

How many packages does the coach have to buy to give each team member 4 pencils?

3 A raisin company donates 96 boxes of raisin snack packs to Grant School. Each box contains 24 snack packs.

There are 384 children at Grant School, and the principal wants to give each child 6 snack packs.

Will there be enough for each child to get 6 packs?

ALTERNATE QUESTION: *How many will be left over or how many more will be needed?*

4 The 24 students in Mrs. Bullock's fourth-grade class are going to make mobiles as gifts for a nursing home. Each mobile will use 10 construction-paper squares that measure 3 inches by 3 inches.

The students figure out that they can make 12 squares from a sheet of paper that measures 9 inches by 12 inches. Mrs. Bullock has 23 sheets of paper.

Does Mrs. Bullock have enough paper for the project?

ALTERNATE QUESTION: *How many sheets will be left over or how many more will be needed?*

5 Mr. Binkley's sixth-grade class is going to have a building contest. Each student will get 50 balsa-wood sticks for a structure. Mr. Binkley is going to participate in the assignment, too.

There are 27 students in the class. Mr. Binkley has 7 packages of sticks with 175 sticks in each package.

Does he have enough sticks for everyone to complete the assignment?

ALTERNATE QUESTION: *How many sticks will be left over or how many more will be needed?*

6 The fifth-grade classes at P.S. 107 are going on a trip to the Museum of Natural History. There are a total of 72 students, 3 teachers, and 3 aides who will be in the group.

The school's corporate sponsor has donated 160 subway tokens for the travelers to use. Each person will use one token going and one token coming back.

Has the sponsor provided enough tokens for everyone?

ALTERNATE QUESTION: *How many tokens will be left over or how many more will be needed?*

MONEY: SET 10

Figuring Profits

1 Tom, Danny, and Patrick decided to sell cookies to raise money for a school trip. They spent $25.00 on ingredients for the cookies, and they each baked 50 cookies.

They sold their cookies for $1.00 each. Tom sold 45 cookies. Danny sold 42 cookies, and Patrick sold 40 cookies.

How much money did they make in profits?

ALTERNATE QUESTION: *How many cookies did they have left over?*

2 Cathy, Joan, and Janna raised money for summer camp by washing cars. They spent $6.00 to buy their supplies and decided to charge $3.00 per car.

Cathy washed 9 cars; Joan washed 12 cars; Janna washed 11 cars.

All together, what was their profit?

3 All 30 families in the Lincoln Apartments held a used book sale to raise money for charity. Each family donated books and contributed $1.00 to place a classified ad in the newspaper.

The families sold hardback books for $1.00 each and paperbacks for 50 cents each. In all, they sold 250 hardback books and 600 paperbacks.

What was their profit?

4 Lee School held a rummage sale to raise money for a new playground. Parents, teachers, and students donated goods to be sold. Five senior citizens volunteered to help out, and the group decided to buy them lunch from the proceeds of their sale.

The group took in $2,495 by the end of the one-day sale. Each senior citizen's lunch cost $5.00.

How much money for the new playground did the group make after costs?

5 Martin Luther King Middle School put on a musical. Production costs totaled $621. They held performances on Friday night and Saturday afternoon. Tickets were $4.00 for adults and $2.00 for children.

On Friday, 331 adults and 307 children came to the musical. On Saturday, 343 adults and 452 children attended.

How much money did they make after expenses?

ALTERNATE QUESTION: *What was the total attendance at both performances?*

6 The snack shop at School 67 is open every day at lunchtime, and the profits support the school. Students can buy granola bars for $.50 or apples for $.30. It costs the school $.40 for the granola bars and $.20 for apples.

During an average week, the shop sells 400 granola bars and 300 apples.

What is the shop's profit during an average week?

Computing Earnings

1 Juanita earned $3.00 an hour doing garden work. She worked for 4 families on her block.

On Saturday, she worked 2 hours in the Cruz garden and 3 hours in the Horowitz garden. On Sunday, she worked 1 hour in the Sahadi garden and 2 hours in the Riley garden.

How much did Juanita earn that week?

2 Chad walks dogs for families in his building. He charges $2.00 an hour per dog.

One Saturday morning, Chad walked Partner and Poncho from 9–10, and he walked Fifi from 10:15–11:15. Then he had lunch. At 12:30 P.M., he walked Rowdy for an hour, and from 1:45–2:45 P.M., he walked Skipper, Mate, and Admiral.

How much did Chad earn that day?

ALTERNATE QUESTION: *Did he earn more after lunch than before lunch, or less? How much?*

3 Leo got an after-school job delivering advertising flyers. He earned $4.00 an hour.

Leo worked 3 days a week from 4 P.M. until 6 P.M. Each of those days, he delivered 200 flyers to homes and apartment buildings.

How much did Leo earn in a two-week period?

4 In December, Thelma offered to shovel snow for her neighbors for $3.00 an hour. Six neighbors told her they'd give her work.

The first week, she worked 1 hour for each neighbor. The second week, she worked a total of 8 hours. The third week, she worked a half hour for each neighbor. The last week of the month, no one needed her services.

How much did Thelma earn in the month of December?

5 Marge started a neighborhood dog-washing business. She charged $5 per dog, which included washing, drying, and light grooming.

She washed Baxter, Chumley, and Doogan every week, and she washed Pepe, Mollie, Rex, and Chester every other week.

How much did Marge make in a four-week period?

6 Howard babysits regularly for three families in his neighborhood, and he charges them $3.00 an hour.

On Thursday he watches Timmy for 2 hours. On Friday he watches the twins, Susie and Sally, for 4 hours. On Saturday, he watches Freddie for 4 hours.

How much does Howard make each week?

MONEY: SET 12

Finding Total Costs

1 Ethan, Todd, and their parents went for dim sum. They ordered 3 large dishes to share, and each had 2 small dishes for themselves.

The large dishes were $4.95 each, and the small dishes were $2.95 each.

How much did the food cost all together?

ALTERNATE QUESTION: *How much was each person's share?*

2 Cinda's family likes to go out for pizza on Saturday nights, and they always order the same thing. Cinda's father and brother order 2 medium pizzas to share, 1 with pepperoni and 1 with mushrooms. Cinda and her mother like to share 1 large vegetarian pizza.

Medium pizzas cost $8.95, while large pizzas cost $12.95.

How much does it cost Cinda's family when they go out for pizza, not including tax?

3 Samantha's grandma and grandpa are going to take her and her 2 brothers to an all-you-can-eat buffet restaurant.

The cost of an adult meal is $7.99, and the cost of a child's meal is $4.99.

How much will it cost for all the meals, not including tax?

4 In 1959, at Bob's Drive-In, a Burger/Shake Special included a hamburger, fries, and a milkshake. A hamburger cost 20 cents, fries cost 15 cents, and a milkshake cost 25 cents.

Four friends went to Bob's for dinner every Friday night, and each one had the Burger/Shake Special.

How much was the total of their bill for one night, not including tax?

5 Dwayne went out for pancakes with his father and sisters. The special that day was a stack of pancakes for $3.25. Side orders of eggs were $.80 per egg.

Everyone ordered the special. Dwayne and his father each had a side order of 2 eggs. Dwayne's 2 sisters had 1 egg each.

How much did it cost the family for their meal, not including tax?

6 Michelle and Roberto went to the ball game with their fathers on Friday night. They decided to have hot dogs and sodas for supper. Jumbo dogs were $3.95, and regular dogs were $2.95. Large sodas were $2.50, and medium sodas were $1.95.

Michelle and Roberto each had a regular dog and a medium soda. Their fathers each had a jumbo dog and a large soda.

How much did the food cost all together?

Spending Money

1 Cameron's grandmother gave him $10.00. He spent $3.25 on a joke book.

Then he spent $1.70 on an energy bar and $1.50 on a plastic whistle.

Does he have enough left over to buy a magazine that costs $2.70?

ALTERNATE QUESTION: *How much will he have left after he buys the magazine?*

2 Ruby's grandmother gave her $20 for her birthday. She deposits $7 in the bank and decides to spend the rest.

Ruby buys a used CD for $3 and a leather bracelet for $5. Then she sees a small bag that she likes. It costs $7.

Does Ruby have enough to buy the bag?

3 Lonnie's godfather gives him $25 as a graduation present. Lonnie wants to buy some old coins and a board game that costs $4.95 plus 25 cents tax.

Lonnie finds packets of old coins at a coin store for $7.95 each plus 40 cents tax.

How many packets of coins can he buy after he buys the game?

ALTERNATE QUESTION: *How much will Lonnie have left after he buys the game and the coins?*

180 Think-Aloud Math Word Problems Scholastic Professional Books

4 By the end of the winter, Thelma had earned $250 shoveling snow on her block. She decided to spend some on her horse and save some for a new saddle.

Thelma bought a used bridle for $95 and a book on grooming horses for $11.

How much does Thelma have left to put toward a new saddle?

5 Yoshi's grandfather gives her $40 for spending three days cleaning out his garage.

Yoshi buys 3 tomato plants, 3 pots, and 2 packages of potting soil so that she can grow tomatoes. The plants cost $2.00 each, and the pots cost 75 cents each. The soil costs $3.95 a package.

How much will Yoshi have left over to buy bamboo stakes and fertilizer?

ALTERNATE QUESTION: *If the stakes and fertilizer cost a total of $9.00, how much will she have left over after buying them?*

6 After six months of washing dogs, Justin had earned $575. He wants to put $500 in the bank but also wants to buy a skateboard, a helmet, and kneepads.

At a block sale, Justin sees a skateboard for $20 and a helmet for $10, so he buys them. Then he buys kneepads, almost new, for $15.

Can Justin put $500 in the bank after all his purchases?

MONEY: SET 14

Planning Purchases

1 Amy is giving a party, and she wants to give noisemakers as favors. She has invited 12 friends to the party and has $5.00 to spend on favors.

She goes to a store and finds noisemakers at 50 cents for a package of 2.

If Amy wants everyone, including herself, to have a noisemaker, how much money will she have to spend?

2 Lamar's family has 2 cats. One day, his brother brings home a stray cat. Their mother says, "Did you think about the cost of feeding another cat?"

Cat food costs $.59 a can, and each cat eats 1 can a day.

How much more will it cost the family to feed the new cat for 1 week?

ALTERNATE QUESTION: *How much will it cost to feed all 3 cats for 1 week?*

3 After school, Ian and his sister stop for snacks at the corner market. They both like fruit chews that cost $.39 each.

Each one eats 1 fruit chew each day after school.

How much money will they spend in 1 week for their snacks?

4 Louise got an aquarium for her birthday and wants to fill it with fish. She can afford to spend $2.00 a week on fish.

The fish she wants cost $.75 each.

How many fish can she buy in 6 weeks?

 5 Paul uses 4 batteries every week for his electronic games.

He buys batteries in packs of 6 for $4.10 a pack, including tax.

How much money will he have to spend on batteries in 1 month?

6 Olivia received $10 as a gift from her grandmother. She wants to buy beads for making jewelry.

At a bead store, Olivia finds beads on sale at $.80 for 2 packages. The tax is 6%.

How many packages can Olivia buy with the money from her grandmother?

Comparing Values

1 The local grocery store has cheese on sale. A four-pound package of cheddar cheese costs $4.00.

A two-pound package of string cheese costs $2.80. A three-pound package of Swiss cheese costs $3.60.

Which cheese is the best buy?

2 Ari goes to the store to buy batteries. He finds them in packs of 2, 4, 6, and 8. Some are on sale.

Packs of 2 and 4 are on sale for $1.69 and $3.29, respectively. Packs of 6 and 8 are on sale for $4.75 and $5.99, respectively.

Which batteries are the best buy?

3 Yvette needs ribbon to wrap holiday presents. At the store, she finds 3 kinds in rolls: gold satin ribbon, red cord, and green ribbon.

The gold ribbon is $.99 for 50 feet. The red cord is $3.00 for 100 feet. The green ribbon is $1.20 for 80 feet.

Which ribbon is the best buy?

4 Roy is in charge of buying candy for the class party. At the store, he finds 3 kinds on sale: chocolate drops at $2.50 a package, mint chews at $3.00 for 2 packages, and caramels at $1.50 a package.

A package of chocolate drops contains 16 ounces. A package of mint chews contains 24 ounces, and a package of caramels contains 14 ounces.

Which candy is the best buy?

5 Elaine's mother gives her $6.00 and tells her to buy some cookies at the grocery store. The store has 2 kinds of cookies on sale: butter cookies and sandwich cookies.

The butter cookies are $2.99 for 2 one-pound boxes, and the sandwich cookies are $4.99 for 2 18-ounce boxes.

Which is the better buy?

6 The grocery store has sweet potatoes at 2 pounds for $.89, yellow potatoes for $.49 per pound, and white potatoes at 3 pounds for $1.29. Chicken is on sale for $.99 a pound.

Jerry buys 2 pounds of chicken and decides to buy a pound of potatoes.

Which kind of potato is the best buy?

MEASUREMENT: SET 16

Comparing Dimensions

1 The Amazon River is 3,900 miles long.

It is 1,552 miles longer than the Mississippi River.

How long is the Mississippi River?

2 An NFL football field must be 120 yards long, while a regulation soccer field must be at least 100 yards long.

An NFL football field is 160 feet wide, while a regulation soccer field must be at least 50 yards wide.

Which is wider: an NFL football field or a soccer field that is the minimum width?

ALTERNATE QUESTION: *Which field has the greater area?*

3 A racquetball court is 20 feet wide and 40 feet long.

A singles tennis court is 7 feet wider and 38 feet longer than a racquetball court.

What are the dimensions of a singles tennis court?

4 Jefferson School's playground is 230 feet by 120 feet.

Adams School's playground is 220 feet by 130 feet.

Which playground has the larger area?

5 Two famous U.S. highways are Route 1 and Route 66. The old Route 1 was 2,390 miles long and went through 15 states.

Route 66, which used to run from Chicago to Los Angeles, was 58 miles longer than Route 1, and it ran through 8 states.

How long was Route 66?

6 Mt. Logan, in Canada's Yukon, is 19,850 feet high.

Mt. McKinley, in Alaska, is 470 feet higher than Mt. Logan.

How high is Mt. McKinley?

MEASUREMENT: SET 17

Finding Cumulative Distances

1 Hank's family decided to climb the mountain outside of town, which is 7,574 feet high. On Saturday, they climbed 1,900 feet, and on Sunday they climbed 1,700 feet.

On Monday, they climbed 1,400 feet, and on Tuesday they climbed 1,300 feet.

How many feet do they still have to climb to reach the top?

2 Jake's family decides to drive to Washington, D.C., which is 1,560 miles from their home. They leave home on Monday morning and drive 371 miles.

On Tuesday, they drive 432 miles, and on Wednesday they drive 393 miles.

How far are they from Washington at the end of the day on Wednesday?

3 Caroline's family likes to explore different routes. One year, they decided to drive the length of three U.S. highways: Route 41, Route 51, and Route 61.

Route 41 is 2,000 miles long. Route 51 is 1,286 miles long, and Route 61 is 1,400 miles long.

If Caroline's family drives 300 miles a day, how long will it take them to drive the lengths of all three highways?

180 Think-Aloud Math Word Problems Scholastic Professional Books

4 Heidi and her family went to Iowa and spent 5 days cycling and camping along country roads. On Monday they rode 42 miles, and on Tuesday they rode 48 miles.

On Wednesday they rode 36 miles, and on Thursday they rode 47 miles. On Thursday night, Heidi said, "We could ride 200 miles this week!"

How many miles will the family have to ride on Friday to reach a total of 200 miles?

5 Joe and Ahmed often take the subway to school. From home, they ride the #3 train 2 miles, then transfer to the #1 train and ride another 3 miles.

One week, they rode the subway every day to and from school, making a total of 5 round-trips.

How many total miles did they ride on the subway that week?

6 Lucy and Marissa liked to walk to and from school. The school was exactly 1 mile from their apartment building.

They walked to and from school every day for 2 weeks, except for 1 day when they took the bus to and from school because it was raining.

How many miles did they walk all together during those 2 weeks?

MEASUREMENT: SET 18

Figuring Total Time to Complete a Project

1 Claudia started making peanut butter cookies at 2:00 P.M. It took her 15 minutes to mix the ingredients for 48 cookies.

She had only one cookie sheet to use, and it held 8 cookies. Each batch took 15 minutes to bake, and it took 5 minutes to get each batch ready for the oven.

When did Claudia finish?

2 George agreed to meet Larry at the city library at 11:30 A.M. to work on their project. He got to the bus stop at 10:15 A.M. and waited 10 minutes for the bus. The bus ride to the subway station took 15 minutes, and he waited 3 minutes for the subway.

The subway ride to the streetcar stop lasted 20 minutes, and he waited 6 minutes for the streetcar. The streetcar ride to the library took 15 minutes.

Did George arrive in time to meet Larry?

3 Nadia opened her new model airplane kit at 9:30 A.M. It took her 35 minutes to glue the pieces together. The directions said to wait 2 hours for the glue to dry.

After waiting the full time, Nadia painted the airplane, which took 20 minutes, and then waited 1 hour for the paint to dry.

What time was it when the paint was dry?

4 It took Dee 10 minutes to pour the plaster of paris into the cat mold and another 10 minutes to wipe off the excess. Then she let the plaster set for 4 hours.

It took her 20 minutes to open the mold and remove the plaster cat, 30 minutes to paint the statue, and 1 hour to let the paint dry. The paint was dry at 4:15 P.M. "Finished at last!" she said.

What time did Dee start her project?

5 Karyn decided to paint a tile for her mother. First she turned on her kiln. Then she got her paints and brushes ready, which took 20 minutes. It took her 45 minutes to paint a design on the tile.

Karyn waited 30 minutes more for the kiln to reach the right temperature and then put the tile in. She fired the tile for 2 hours, let it cool for 3 hours, and took the finished tile out of the kiln at 6 P.M.

What time did Karyn start her project?

6 Toby made his father a birthday cake. At 9 A.M., he mixed the ingredients and poured the batter in the pan. Then he realized that he had forgotten to turn on the oven.

He turned the oven on at 9:30 A.M. and waited 15 minutes for it to heat up to the right temperature. Then he put in the cake and let it bake for 25 minutes. He let the cake cool for 1 hour and then frosted it, which took 25 minutes.

What time did Toby finish?

Figuring Travel Time and Distance

1 Rocky's family is going to drive from their home near St. Louis, Missouri, to her grandmother's home near Chicago, Illinois, a distance of 290 miles.

Rocky's mother is the driver, and she averages 50 miles an hour.

How many hours will it take them to get to Chicago?

ALTERNATE QUESTION: *How many hours and minutes will it take them to get to Chicago?*

2 Kelly and her family plan to drive to Yosemite National Park in California from their home near San Antonio, Texas, a distance of 1,676 miles.

The family has 14 days for its vacation and wants to spend 6 days at the park.

How many miles will they have to drive each day to keep to their schedule?

3 Rashid and his family are going to Honolulu, Hawaii, from their home in Seattle, Washington, which is a distance of 2,680 air miles.

When the family gets on the plane, Rashid hears the pilot say they will average 600 miles per hour.

How long will it take to fly to Honolulu?

4 Bretta and her family want to drive from Minneapolis, Minnesota, to Disney World in Orlando, Florida, a distance of 1,572 miles.

Bretta's mother says, "The bus will get us there in 3 days."

How many miles will the bus cover each day?

5 Tad's family wants to see the Grand Canyon in Arizona. They decide to rent a car and drive there from their home in Boston, Massachusetts, then fly back.

Tad's father says, "The driving distance is 2,629 miles. I think we can do 400 miles a day."

How many days will it take them to get from Boston to the Grand Canyon?

6 The sixth-grade class at Davis School is going to Washington, D.C., a distance of 720 miles from their school near Birmingham, Alabama.

The group is taking a special bus that will cover 360 miles a day.

How many days will they be on the road all together?

Determining the Amount Needed

1 Randy's mother asks him to figure out how much paint they need to cover the walls of the family room in their new house.

All 4 walls are 8 feet high. Of the 4 walls, 2 are 12 feet long and 2 are 24 feet long.

If 1 quart of paint covers 10 square feet, how many quarts will the family need for the project?

ALTERNATE QUESTION: *If the paint is sold only in gallons, how many gallons will they need?*

2 Milton's family is putting new carpet in two bedrooms and part of a hallway, and he wants to help with the estimates.

One room is 10 feet by 13 feet, and the other room is 9 feet by 12 feet. The hallway is 5 feet long and 3 feet wide.

How many square feet of carpet will the family need to buy?

ALTERNATE QUESTION: *If carpet is sold by the yard, how many square yards will they need?*

3 Serena is in charge of buying balloons to decorate the classroom for a party. The class wants to string 2 rows of balloons along the windows.

The wall of windows is 36 feet long, and Serena figures they'll need to have a balloon every 4 inches.

How many balloons will Serena need to buy?

4 Tina is helping her mother decorate the community center for a New Year's party. The room is 25 feet wide and 50 feet long.

They are going to put bunting on the walls all around the room. The bunting is sold 10 feet to a package. A package costs $4.95.

How many packages will they need for the job?

ALTERNATE QUESTION: *How much will all the bunting cost, not including tax?*

5 Savannah is planting a flower garden. The area is 10 feet by 20 feet. She wants to make a border of lobelia on the perimeter.

Lobelia plants come in flats of 6. They need to be planted 6 inches apart.

How many flats does Savannah need?

ALTERNATE QUESTION: *How many plants will she use all together?*

6 Donovan wants to decorate one wall of his room with posters. The wall is 9 feet high and 12 feet long.

The posters he wants to use are 36 inches high and 24 inches long.

How many posters does he need to cover the entire wall?

MEASUREMENT: SET 21

Finding Dimensions of a Surface

1 Bob's family is building a new house with 3 bedrooms, a living room, and a family room. Bob's room will be 12 feet wide.

Bob's room is going to be twice as long as it is wide.

What will be the perimeter of Bob's room?

ALTERNATE QUESTION: *What will be the area of Bob's room?*

2 The residents of the Casa Luja Apartments want to plant grass in their two shared courtyards.

The first courtyard is 10 feet wide and 26 feet long. The second is 20 feet wide and 30 feet long.

What is the total area that needs to be seeded with grass?

3 The Ames Retirement Home invited 4 third-grade classes to display their art projects in the dining room. The room is 45 feet wide and 60 feet long and has no windows.

There are 2 doors into the room, each with an opening 6 feet wide. The art must be placed in a 3-foot high strip of space along the walls.

What is the total length of the display space the children will be able to use?

4 Mrs. Kwan's class is going to paint murals in the foyer of their school. There are 2 walls in the foyer that can be painted.

Each foyer wall is 12 feet high and 15 feet long.

What is the total area to be painted with murals?

5 McKinley School needs new fences in the front and back of the building. Each area will be fenced on only 3 sides because the 300-foot-long school building will form the fourth side of each fenced area.

The front area to be fenced is 300 feet by 120 feet. The back area is 300 feet by 180 feet.

How many feet of fencing will be needed all together?

6 The parents of Roosevelt School are going to put in a new three-part playground outside the kindergarten rooms.

There will be a 12- by 12-foot area of grass, a 6- by 20-foot area of concrete, and an 8- by 12-foot area of sand.

What is the total area of the new playground?

Determining Largest Fractional Amount

1 Two classes had a party. One class brought a chocolate cake, and the other class brought a carrot cake. Each cake was cut into 24 pieces.

At the end of the party, $\frac{1}{4}$ of the chocolate cake was not eaten and $\frac{1}{3}$ of the carrot cake was not eaten.

Was there more chocolate cake or carrot cake left over?

ALTERNATE QUESTION: *How many pieces of each kind of cake were left over?*

2 Mr. Carter brought a large pizza for the after-school chess club. There were 4 students in the club.

Mr. Carter said, "You may each have $\frac{1}{2}$ of $\frac{1}{2}$ of this pizza, or you may each have $\frac{2}{8}$ of the pizza."

Which is more?

3 Margo was cutting paper strips for a project. Each strip had to be less than 1 inch wide.

The directions said, "The blue strips must be $\frac{5}{8}$ of an inch wide. The yellow strips must be $\frac{1}{2}$ an inch wide. The red strips must be $\frac{1}{3}$ of an inch wide."

Which color strip is the widest?

ALTERNATE QUESTION: *How wide is the strip that can be made by putting a blue strip, a yellow strip, and a red strip side by side?*

180 Think-Aloud Math Word Problems Scholastic Professional Books

4 Mrs. Lindsay bought 1 pound of banana chips for her 4 children. "I want to give each of you an equal amount," she said. "Help me figure out how much I should give each of you."

"Should I give each of you $\frac{2}{8}$ of a pound, $\frac{2}{6}$ of a pound, or $\frac{1}{5}$ of a pound of chips?"

Which is the correct amount?

5 Amos entered a writing contest and won first prize. He got his choice of 3 bags of candy.

The first package contained $\frac{1}{2}$ a pound. The second package contained $\frac{3}{8}$ of a pound. The third package contained $\frac{4}{5}$ of a pound. Amos wanted the package with the most candy.

Which one should Amos choose?

6 Mr. Litton's class voted on their favorite foods. Mr. Litton and all 29 students participated.

Of the group, $\frac{2}{5}$ liked pizza best, $\frac{1}{6}$ liked tacos best, $\frac{1}{3}$ liked spaghetti best, and $\frac{1}{10}$ liked grilled cheese sandwiches best.

Which food got the most votes?

ALTERNATE QUESTION: *How many votes did each food get?*

Finding Common Denominators

1 Tatiana is pasting strips of ribbon on paper to make a greeting card. The widths of the ribbons are $\frac{1}{8}$ inch, $\frac{1}{3}$ inch, $\frac{3}{8}$ inch, $\frac{1}{2}$ inch, and $\frac{1}{4}$ inch.

The ribbons are all different colors. Tatiana wants to use 3 colors to make a 1-inch strip of ribbon on the card.

How can she combine ribbons to have the width she wants?

2 Mac has 6 pieces of scrap wood to use in a project. Each piece is less than 2 inches long.

One piece is $1\frac{1}{4}$ inches long, another is $1\frac{1}{2}$ inches long, and a third piece is $\frac{1}{2}$ inch long. The other 3 pieces are each 1 inch long.

How many lengths of exactly 2 inches can Mac make from the scraps he has?

3 Jessica is pasting pieces of colored paper on a box to decorate it. All the paper strips are $\frac{1}{2}$ inch wide. The box is 8 inches long and 4 inches wide.

The yellow strips are $3\frac{1}{2}$ inches long. The blue strips are $4\frac{1}{2}$ inches long, and the red strips are $1\frac{1}{2}$ inches long.

How many different ways can Jessica create a strip that is 8 inches long without cutting any of the strips?

4 Dermot has 5 kinds of flour left over after making bread. He has $\frac{1}{2}$ cup of barley flour, $\frac{3}{4}$ cup of wheat flour, $\frac{1}{4}$ cup of oat flour, $1\frac{1}{2}$ cups of rye flour, and 2 cups of graham flour.

Dermot's mother says, "You can make breadsticks with the leftovers. The recipe calls for only 2 cups of flour. You can mix any kinds of flour together."

How can Dermot get exactly 2 cups of flour from his leftovers?

5 Breanna needs 2 cups of beans to make bean soup.

She has $\frac{1}{2}$ cup of pinto beans, $\frac{3}{4}$ cup of navy beans, $\frac{1}{4}$ cup of black beans, $\frac{1}{2}$ cup of lima beans, and $1\frac{1}{2}$ cups of garbanzo beans.

What combinations of beans can she use when she makes the soup?

6 Ross is helping his mother make a candy mix. They have $2\frac{1}{2}$ cups of jelly beans, $1\frac{1}{2}$ cups of gumdrops, and 1 cup of peppermints.

They want to make 2 bowls of candy mix with the same amounts of each kind of candy in each bowl.

How can they do it?

Adding Fractions

1 Nigel is making holiday cookies. His recipe calls for $\frac{1}{2}$ pound of raisins.

The recipe also calls for $\frac{1}{4}$ pound of dates and $\frac{1}{8}$ pound of dried apricots.

How much dried fruit will he put into the cookies in all?

2 At the farmers' market, plums, oranges, and apples are selling for $1.00 a pound.

Megan bought $1\frac{1}{2}$ pounds of plums, $\frac{3}{4}$ pound of apples, and 2 pounds of oranges.

How much fruit did she buy in all?

ALTERNATE QUESTION: *How much did Megan's purchases cost in all?*

3 At the hardware store, $\frac{1}{2}$-inch nails, $\frac{3}{4}$-inch nails, and $\frac{5}{8}$-inch nails are all on sale for $.89 a pound.

Tess bought $\frac{1}{4}$ pound of $\frac{1}{2}$-inch nails, $\frac{1}{2}$ pound of $\frac{3}{4}$-inch nails, and $\frac{3}{4}$ pound of $\frac{5}{8}$-inch nails.

What was the total weight of her purchases?

180 Think-Aloud Math Word Problems Scholastic Professional Books

4 The grocery store has a sale on dried beans. Pinto beans are $.60 a pound. Kidney beans are $.80 a pound. Black beans are $.90 a pound.

Greg measures out $\frac{2}{3}$ pound of pinto beans, $\frac{1}{4}$ pound of kidney beans, and $\frac{1}{3}$ pound of black beans.

How many pounds of beans does he have in all?

ALTERNATE QUESTION: *How much will the beans cost all together?*

5 Mariana is making bread that contains 4 different kinds of flour.

The recipe calls for $2\frac{1}{2}$ cups of wheat flour, $\frac{3}{4}$ cup of barley flour, $\frac{1}{2}$ cup of oat flour, and $\frac{1}{4}$ cup of rye flour.

How much flour will Mariana use all together?

6 Marlo is making snacks that contain 3 kinds of dried fruit and 3 kinds of nuts. He gets out a mixing bowl.

In the bowl, he first puts 2 cups of walnuts, $\frac{3}{4}$ cup of almonds, and $1\frac{1}{2}$ cups of pecans. Then he adds 1 cup of dates, $\frac{3}{4}$ cup of figs, and $\frac{1}{2}$ cup of apricots.

How many cups of fruit-nut mix does Marlo have in all?

Adding and Subtracting Fractions

1 Vickie's parents served 6 pizzas to their guests one night. Each pizza was cut into 12 pieces.

The family and guests ate all of 2 pizzas, $\frac{1}{2}$ each of the next 2 pizzas, and $\frac{2}{3}$ each of the last 2 pizzas.

How many pieces were left over?

2 Robin helped her mother make 6 pies for the family's holiday party. They cut each pie into 6 pieces.

At the party, the relatives ate all of 2 pies, $\frac{1}{2}$ each of 2 more pies, and $\frac{2}{3}$ of each of the last 2 pies.

How many pieces of pie were left over?

3 Simon made a pan of chocolate fudge and a pan of vanilla fudge. He cut each pan of fudge into 24 pieces.

Simon's friends ate $\frac{1}{4}$ of the chocolate fudge and $\frac{1}{3}$ of the vanilla fudge.

How many pieces of fudge were left over?

180 Think-Aloud Math Word Problems   Scholastic Professional Books

4 Jeremy's father bought 6 cases of soft drinks for a family barbecue. Each case held 6 packages of 6 cans.

At the barbecue, the family drank only $\frac{1}{4}$ of the soda.

How many cans were left over?

5 Deanna put together small cups of jelly beans to use for favors at her birthday party. She put 10 jelly beans in each cup.

At the party, 2 of the guests each ate $\frac{1}{2}$ of their jellybeans, and 2 others ate $\frac{2}{5}$ of theirs. Deanna ate $\frac{1}{5}$ of hers. Deanna said, "Let's count how many we have left!"

How many jelly beans were left all together?

6 Mrs. Grundy bought 6 dozen cookies for her students on the last day of school.

There were 24 students in the class. Half of the students ate 2 cookies each. One-fourth of the students ate 3 cookies each, and one-fourth ate 4 cookies each.

How many cookies were left over?

FRACTIONS AND PERCENTS: SET 26

Converting Between Fractions and Percents

1 A class of 32 students surveyed themselves on how often they watch television. They came up with 4 categories.

One-fourth of the students watch TV less than 1 hour a day. Half of the students watch between 1 and 2 hours a day. One-eighth of the students watch TV between 2 and 3 hours a day, and one-eighth watch TV more than 3 hours a day.

What percentage of students is there in each category?

2 Mrs. Conner baked 100 cookies for her guests, making an equal number of each of 4 kinds.

The guests ate $\frac{2}{5}$ of the oatmeal cookies, $\frac{1}{5}$ of the peanut butter cookies, $\frac{1}{5}$ of the lemon cookies, and $\frac{3}{5}$ of the walnut cookies.

What percentage of cookies was left over?

3 There are 64 units in the Hillside Apartments.

Of all the apartments, $\frac{3}{8}$ have views of the river and downtown, $\frac{3}{8}$ have views of the mountains and downtown, and $\frac{1}{4}$ have views only of the inner courtyard.

What percentage of the apartments has a view of downtown?

4 In a school, 19% of the students are in kindergarten, 21% in grade 1, 20% in grade 2, and 15% in grade 3.

The fourth grade has 16% of the students, while the fifth grade has 9% of the students.

What fraction of the total student body is in kindergarten through grade 3?

5 Eric and Rosemary made a Halloween mix of 4 different kinds of wrapped candy. There were 200 pieces in all.

The mix was 35% toffee, 25% peppermint, and equal percentages of licorice and butterscotch.

What fraction of the mix was made up of butterscotch candy?

ALTERNATE QUESTION: *How many pieces of butterscotch candy were in the mix?*

6 Everyone in Mrs. Hensen's fifth-grade class of 32 students likes one of three sports best of all.

Soccer is the favorite of 16 of the students, while 12 like softball the best and 4 like tennis the best.

What percentage of the class likes each sport?

Detecting Sequences

1 Sharon received 8 beads for her eighth birthday and 16 beads for her ninth birthday.

For her tenth birthday, Sharon received 32 beads.

At this rate, how many beads will Sharon receive for her eleventh birthday?

2 Oscar bought a bag of 144 food pellets for his pet rat, Roger. The first day, Roger ate 21 pellets. The next day, he ate 17 pellets.

The third day, Roger ate 13 pellets.

At that rate, how many pellets will Roger eat on the fifth day?

3 Louis loves to read. On March 1, he checked out 15 books from the library, and on March 8, he checked out 18 books.

On March 15, he checked out 21 books.

At this rate, how many books will Louis check out of the library on March 29?

180 Think-Aloud Math Word Problems   Scholastic Professional Books

4 Raul raises fish. His grandfather said to him, "I will give you 2 fish this year for your tenth birthday."

"Then for your eleventh birthday, I'll give you 6 fish," said his grandfather, "and for your twelfth birthday, I'll give you 18 fish."

"At this rate," Raul's grandfather continued, "how many fish will I give you for your fourteenth birthday?" What did Raul answer?

5 Augusta loves to practice hitting golf balls on the driving range. One Saturday, she hit 42 balls, and the next Saturday, she hit 54 balls.

The third Saturday, she hit 66 balls, and the fourth Saturday, she hit 78.

At this rate, how many balls will Augusta hit on the seventh Saturday?

6 The Roxy Theatre sold 403 tickets one Saturday night. On Sunday night they sold 382 tickets.

On Monday night, they sold 361 tickets.

If they continue selling tickets at this rate, how many will they sell the next Friday night?

Using Rate to Determine Total

1 Mike agrees to fold pizza boxes at the take-out pizza place his father manages. Mike's father needs 100 boxes folded by 6 P.M.

Mike can fold 3 boxes in 1 minute.

If Mike starts at 5:15 P.M., can he fold the number his father needs in time?

2 Mrs. Casey is in charge of making sandwiches in the lunchroom. She can make 4 sandwiches in 2 minutes.

One Monday, she must make 400 sandwiches by 12:00 noon.

What time does she need to start?

3 To stay in shape, Vince swims laps in the pool at his health club. He can swim 1 lap in 1 minute, 30 seconds.

One Saturday at 9 A.M., Vince decides to swim 50 laps.

How long will it take him to swim that number of laps?

ALTERNATE QUESTION: *What time will he be finished?*

4 Valerie and Pauline like to make pretzels. Once the dough is ready, they can get 4 pretzels ready for baking every minute.

One day, they decide to make 6 dozen pretzels and make enough dough for that many.

How long does it take them to get 6 dozen pretzels ready for baking?

5 A youth club holds a car wash to raise money. They divide into two teams. Each team can wash a car in 15 minutes.

Everyone works from 9 A.M. to 12:00 noon, and they have a constant stream of customers the entire time.

How many cars do they wash in all that morning?

6 A class toured a candy factory and saw a machine that makes 400 gumdrops every minute.

The gumdrop machine is in operation from 9 A.M. to 4 P.M. every day.

How many gumdrops can the machine turn out in 1 hour?

ALTERNATE QUESTION: *How many gumdrops can the machine turn out in 1 day?*

Finding the Average

1 Two sisters and two brothers like to grow vegetables. One year they all decided to grow tomatoes, and each planted 3 tomato plants.

By the end of the summer, Ann had picked 99 tomatoes from her plants, and Bill had picked 87 tomatoes from his. Carol had picked 115 tomatoes from her plants, and Dave had picked 107 from his.

What was the average number of tomatoes harvested per person?

2 Burt got a new outdoor thermometer that ranged from –20 to 120 degrees Fahrenheit.

Burt checked the temperature at noon every day for a week and got the following readings: 67, 68, 74, 77, 69, 65, and 63.

What was the average daily noon temperature that week?

3 Chester rides the public bus to school every morning. One week, he counted the number of people who were on his bus at 8:30 A.M.

On Monday, he counted 49, on Tuesday, 53, on Wednesday, 57, on Thursday, 55, and on Friday, 46.

How many people were on the bus, on average, each morning?

4 Enid's cat had 7 kittens, and Enid weighed them when they were 2 weeks old.

Two kittens weighed 12 ounces each, and two others weighed 14 ounces each. The others weighed 10 ounces, 13 ounces, and 16 ounces.

What was the average weight of the kittens?

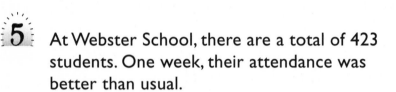

5 At Webster School, there are a total of 423 students. One week, their attendance was better than usual.

On Monday, 408 came to school. On Tuesday, 416 were there. On Wednesday and Thursday, 420 were in school. On Friday, 411 were there.

What was the average daily attendance that week?

6 Mr. Singh's students measured their heights and made a bar graph to show the results.

There were 5 children who were 4 feet 9 inches tall, 4 who were 4 feet 11 inches tall, 3 who were 5 feet tall, 3 who were 5 feet 2 inches tall, 2 who were 5 feet 4 inches tall, and 1 who was 5 feet 5 inches tall.

What was the average height of the students in the group?

Logical Reasoning

1 Volunteers planted 10 maple trees across the front of Franklin School. They left 2 maple trees in Mr. Robson's truck because there wasn't enough room to plant them.

Then the volunteers went to McClure School and planted 6 oak trees in front and the remaining maples on the south side. At that point, the truck was empty.

How many trees were in the truck when they started?

2 Mr. Kepler bought a subway ticket good for 10 one-way rides. After he had used up 6 rides, he absentmindedly left the ticket at home and bought another 10-ride ticket on the way to work.

After he had used up 5 rides on the new ticket, he absentmindedly left that ticket at work, so he bought another 10-ride ticket for the ride home.

When he got home that day, how many unused rides did he have in all?

3 Naomi checked out 9 books from the library one Saturday morning. She finished 2 books that week and started 3 more.

The next Saturday, she returned all the books except for the 3 she was reading and checked out 7 more. On Monday, she returned 2 books and checked out 1 more.

How many books did Naomi have at home on Monday night?

4 Ira forgot his lunch money on Monday and borrowed 75 cents from Julius to buy a school lunch. The next day, he again forgot his money and again borrowed lunch money from Julius.

On Wednesday, Ira paid Julius back. On Thursday, Julius had to borrow lunch money from Ira, and on Friday, Ira had to borrow lunch money from Julius.

How much did Julius owe Ira on Friday?

5 The Wesleys decided to donate all 80 of their paperbacks to two neighborhood used-book sales. On Saturday morning, they took half the books to the first sale and bought 16 books while they were there.

On Saturday afternoon, they took half the remaining books they had planned to donate to the second sale, leaving the other half behind by accident. At that sale, they bought 23 books.

How many paperbacks did they have at the end of the day?

6 Kia buys a bag of apples at the farmers' market. On the way home, she gives 2 apples each to 2 friends she meets, and she gives 1 to Officer Smith, who is on duty in the neighborhood. When Officer Smith's dog, Max, knocks Marty's bag down, 3 apples roll into the street and are lost.

Kia gives 2 apples to the lady next door. Then she heads home and counts the apples left in the bag. She has 13.

How many apples did she buy at the farmer's market?

Solutions and Answers

Here are the answers to the questions, along with the steps taken to solve each problem. Students may take a different approach to solving a problem than is explained here.

ADDITION AND SUBTRACTION

Set 1 (pages 12–13)

1. 23 watches + 4 more on Saturday = 27
   27 + (2 × 3) = 33 watches
   ALTERNATE: 4 × $2 = $8; 6 × $1 = $6; $8 + $6 = $14

2. 42 + 12 + 9 + 14 = 77 stamps purchased
   100 − 77 = 23 stamps needed

3. 440 + (4 × 5) + (3 × 5) + (2 × 5) + (2 × 5) = 495 cards purchased
   500 − 495 = 5 cards left
   No, Shawn did not reach his goal.

4. 28 (already owned) + 2 + 4 + 6 + 5 = 45 magnets
   ALTERNATE: 2 + 4 + 6 + 5 = 17 magnets

5. 3 + 6 + (3 × 2) + (4 + 4) = 23 waffles

6. Boris's total: 500 + 350 + 200 + 600 = 1,650
   Eddie's total: 450 + 520 + 180 + 570 = 1,720
   Eddie had the highest overall total.

Set 2 (pages 14–15)

1. 2 (Monday) + 5 (Tuesday) = 7
   7 (Wednesday) + 9 (Thursday) = 16 + 2 (Friday) = 18
   7 + 18 = 25 cents

2. Group 1: 24 (Monday) + 26 (Tuesday) = 50 taxis
   Group 2: 7 (Monday) + 6 (Tuesday) = 13 buses
   Group 3: 31 (Monday) + 34 (Tuesday) = 65 trucks
   ALTERNATE: 50 + 13 + 65 = 128 vehicles

3. Alexa: (4 × $1) × 10 = $40
   Barker: (4 × $1) × 12 = $48
   Crystal: (5 × $1) × 20 = $100
   $40 + $48 + $100 = $188

4. Monday = 1; Tuesday = 2; Wednesday = 3;
   Thursday = 2; Friday = 1
   1 + 2 + 3 + 2 + 1 = 9 inches

5. Monday: 20 pencils, 6 erasers
   Wednesday: 10 pencils, 12 erasers
   Friday: 40 pencils, 24 erasers
   20 + 10 + 40 = 70 pencils; 6 + 12 + 24 = 42 erasers
   ALTERNATE: 70 × $.10 = $7.00; 42 × $.25 = $10.50;
   $7.00 + $10.50 = $17.50

6. Week 1 = 98; Week 2 = 198; Week 3 = 99; Week 4 = 107 bars

98 + 198 + 99 + 107 = 502 bars sold
ALTERNATE: 502 × $.50 = $251 total sales of bars

Set 3 (pages 16–17)

1. Barry: 56 + 9 − 12 = 53 marbles
   Brian: 47 − 9 + 12 = 50 marbles

2. Carmen: $7.36 − $1.25 − $1.40 + $1.40 = $6.11
   Christine: $8.69 + $1.25 − $1.40 − $1.80 = $6.74

3. Lost tennis balls: 8 + 5 + 3 = 16
   40 − 16 = 24 + 4 (found on court) = 28 tennis balls
   ALTERNATE: 40 − 28 = 12 tennis balls lost

4. Angelica: 63 − 13 + 7 = 57 charms
   Brittany: 49 + 13 − 7 = 55 charms
   ALTERNATE: Angelica had 2 more charms.

5. $2.39 + $1.00 + $.03 + $.10 = $3.52
   ALTERNATE: $3.50 − 2.39 = $1.11

6. 28 × 5 = 140 balloons to start
   140 − (24 + 11) = 105 left after losses
   105 + 10 (from Ms. Penny's desk) = 115 balloons

Set 4 (pages 18–19)

1. 1993 (Diana's birth) − 1939 (Grandma's birth) = 54 years old

2. 1985 + 12 = 1997 (year he sold the car)
   1997 − 1957 = 40 years old

3. 18 − 9 = 9 years old

4. 1994 − 2 = 1992 (year Sumi is born)
   2000 − 1992 = 8 years old

5. 1995 − 1942 = 53 years old (grandfather's age)
   1995 − 1968 = 27 years old (father's age)

6. 2003 − 1960 = 43 years old
   ALTERNATE: 2003 − 1936 = 67 years

Set 5 (pages 20–21)

1. 2000 − 191 = 1809
2. 1938 − 37 = 1901
3. 1800 − 57 = 1743
4. 1954 − 18 = 1936
5. 1881 − 25 = 1856
6. 1791 + 9 = 1800

MULTIPLICATION AND DIVISION

Set 6 (pages 22–23)

1. $6 \times 6 = 36$ granddaughters
   $6 \times 2 = 12$ grandsons
   $36 + 12 = 48$ grandchildren

2. $3 \times 12 = 36$ cookies made each day in one class
   $4 \times 36 = 144$ cookies made each day by all classes
   $5 \times 144 = 720$ cookies made in all

3. $2 (2 \times 12) + 2 (3 \times 12) = 48 + 72 = 120$ books
   $2 (3 \times 12) + 2 (4 \times 12) = 72 + 96 = 168$ books
   $120 + 168 = 288$ books; yes, they reached their goal.

4. $18 \times 5 = 90; 20 \times 5 = 100; 25 \times 5 = 125$
   $90 + 100 + 125 = 315$; yes, they got their pizza.

5. $(2 \times 52) + (2 \times 70) + (2 \times 74) + (2 \times 82) = 556$
   mittens

6. $(15 \times 5) + (25 \times 4) = 175$ minutes for weeks 1 and 2
   $(32 \times 4) + (20 \times 4) = 208$ minutes for weeks 3 and 4
   $175 + 208 = 383$; Takisha's mother stayed within her limit.

Set 7 (pages 24–25)

1. 8 slices $\times 4$ pizzas $= 32$ slices
   5 people $\times 4$ slices $= 20$ slices
   32 slices available $- 20$ slices eaten $= 12$ slices left over

2. 4 campers $\times 2$ bars $= 8$ bars per day
   24 bars $\div 8$ bars per day $= 3$ days

3. 24 pieces $+ 15$ pieces $+ 18$ pieces $= 57$ pieces
   57 pieces $\div 3$ boys $= 19$ pieces each
   ALTERNATE: 3 bags $\times \$2.50 = \$7.50$

4. 2 cakes $\times 24$ pieces $= 48$ pieces in all
   48 pieces $\div 20$ students $= 2$ pieces each
   ALTERNATE: There are 8 pieces left over, so 8 people
   could have another piece.

5. $26 \div 4 = 6$ pretzels each (2 left over)
   $35 \div 4 = 8$ crackers each (3 left over)
   The boys gave Ravi's mother 2 pretzels and 3 crackers.

6. $5 - 2 = 3$ pieces; Carlene and Danielle each have 3
   pieces.
   Suki and Ana each have 2 pieces (each got 1 from
   Carlene, 1 from Danielle).

Set 8 (pages 26–27)

1. $\$675 \div 3$ classes $= \$225$ per class

2. $25 + 22 + 28 + 3 + 7 = 85$ people
   $85 \div 17 = 5$ buses needed
   ALTERNATE: $5 \times \$34 = \$170; \$170 \div 85 = \$2$ per person

3. $\$2 \times 28 = \$56$, so \$2 per person is enough.

4. Total number people $= 30$ (29 students $+ 1$ teacher)
   $\$45 \div 30 = \$1.50$ per person

5. $\$5 + \$3 + \$2 = \$10$ per person
   $\$10 \times 5 = \$50$ for all 5 boys
   $\$50 \div 4 = \$12.50$ per friend

6. $\$54.95 + \$4.45 = \$59.40$
   $\$59.40 \div 4 = \$14.85$ per girl

Set 9 (pages 28–29)

1. 26 students $\times 20$ sheets $= 520$ sheets
   No, 500 sheets is not enough.

2. 8 students $\times 4$ pencils $= 32$ pencils needed
   $12 \times 3 = 36$ pencils in 3 packages. 3 packages needed

3. $96 \times 24 = 2,304$ total snack packs
   $2,304 \div 384 = 6$; yes, there will be exactly enough.
   ALTERNATE: There will be none left over.

4. 24 students $\times 10$ squares $= 240$ squares needed
   23 sheets $\times 12$ squares $= 276$ squares available
   Yes, she has enough.
   ALTERNATE: 36 squares, or 3 sheets left over

5. $28 \times 50 = 1,400$ sticks needed
   $7 \times 175 = 1,225$ sticks available
   No, there are not enough for the assignment.
   ALTERNATE: An additional package of 175 sticks is
   needed.

6. $72 + 3 + 3 = 78$ people
   $78 \times 2 = 156$ tokens needed
   Yes, the sponsor has provided enough.
   ALTERNATE: $160 - 156 = 4$ tokens left over

MONEY

Set 10 (pages 30–31)

1. $45 + 42 + 40 = 127$ cookies
   $127 \times \$1 = \$127$
   $\$127 - \$25$ (costs) $= \$102$ profit
   ALTERNATE: $150 - 127 = 23$ cookies left over

2. $9 + 12 + 11 = 32$ cars washed
   32 cars $\times \$3 = \$96$
   $\$96 - \$6$ (supplies) $= \$90$ profit

3. 250 hardbacks $\times \$1 = \$250$
   600 paperbacks $\times \$.50 = \$300$
   $\$250 + \$300 = \$550$
   $\$550 - \$30$ (for the ad) $= \$520$ profit

4. 5 seniors $\times \$5 = \$25$
   $\$2,495 - \$25$ (lunch) $= \$2,470$ profit for playground

5. $\$4 \times (331 + 343) = \$2,696$
   $\$2 \times (307 + 452) = \$1,518$
   $\$2,696 + \$1,518 = \$4,214$
   $\$4214 - \$621 = \$3593$ left
   ALTERNATE: $331 + 307 + 343 + 452 = 1,433$ total
   attendance

6. 400 × $.50 = $200
400 × $.40 = $160
$200 − $160 = $40 profit on bars
300 × $.30 = $90
300 × $.20 = $60
$90 − $60 = $30 profit on apples
$40 +$ 30 = $70 total profit

Set 11 (pages 32–33)

1. Saturday: 2 + 3 = 5 hours; 5 hours × $3 = $15
Sunday: 1 + 2 = 3 hours; 3 hours × $3 = $9
$15 + $9 = $24

2. $4 for Partner and Poncho
$2 for Fifi and $2 for Rowdy
$6 for Skipper, Mate, and Admiral
$4 + $2 + $2 + $6 = $14 for the day
ALTERNATE: He earned $2 more after lunch than he earned before lunch.

3. Leo worked 2 hours a day, 3 days a week, making $4 an hour.
2 × 3 = 6 hours a week; 6 hours × $4 = $24 a week
$24 + $24 = $48

4. Week 1: 6 hours × $3 = $18; week 2: 8 hours × $3 = $24
Week 3: .5 hours × 6 = 3 hours; 3 hours × $3 = $9
$18 + $24 + $9 = $51

5. $5 × 3 dogs = $15 (every week); $15 × 4 = $60 in 4 weeks
$5 × 4 dogs = $20 (every other week); $20 × 2 = $40 in 4 weeks
$60 + $40 = $100

6. 2 hours + 4 hours + 4 hours = 10 hours work
10 hours × $3 per hour = $30 a week

Set 12 (pages 34–35)

1. 3 × $4.95 = $14.85 (total for shared dishes)
8 × $2.95 = $23.60 (total for individual dishes)
$14.85 + $23.60 = $38.45
ALTERNATE: $38.45 ÷ 4 = $9.61 per person

2. 2 × $8.95 = $17.90
$17.90 + $12.95 = $30.85

3. $7.99 × 2 = $15.98 (cost of 2 adult meals)
$4.99 × 3 = $14.97 (cost of 3 child meals)
$15.98 + $14.97 = $30.95

4. $.20 + $.15 + $.25 = $.60
$.60 × 4 people = $2.40

5. $3.25 × 4 = $13 (cost of specials)
$.80 × 6 = $4.80 (cost of eggs)
$13.00 + $4.80 = $17.80

6. $2.95 + $1.95 = $4.90; $4.90 × 2 = $9.80 (cost for boys)

$3.95 + $2.50 = $6.45; $6.45 × 2 = $12.90 (cost for fathers)
$9.80 + $12.90 = $22.70

Set 13 (pages 36–37)

1. $10.00 − $3.25 − $1.70 − $1.50 = $3.55 left
Yes, he has enough to buy a magazine for $2.70.
ALTERNATE: $3.55 − $2.70 = $.85

2. $20.00 − $7.00 = $13 to spend
$3.00 + $5.00 = $8 spent; $13.00 − $8.00 = $5
Ruby does not have enough for the bag.

3. $4.95 + $.25 = $5.20 (for the board game)
$25.00 − $5.20 = $19.80 (left to spend on coins)
$7.95 + $.40 = $8.35 for 1 packet of coins
3 will cost more than $24; 2 will cost less than $17.00;
Lonnie can buy 2.
ALTERNATE: $19.80 − $16.70 = $3.10

4. $95.00 + $11.00 = $106 for bridle and book
$250.00 − $106.00 = $144

5. 3 × $2.00 = $6 (cost of plants)
3 × $.75 = $2.25 (cost of pots)
2 × $3.95 = $7.90 (cost of soil)
$6.00 + $2.25 + $7.90 = $16.15 (cost of all three)
$40.00 − $16.15 = $23.85
ALTERNATE: $23.85 − $9.00 = $14.85 left over

6. $20 + $10 + $15 = $45 (total for purchases)
$575 − $45 = $530
Yes, he can put $500 in the bank.

Set 14 (pages 38–39)

1. Amy needs 13 favors (12 guests and herself).
Favors come in packages of 2, so she must buy an even number (14).
14 favors ÷ 2 = 7 packages
7 × $.50 = $3.50

2. $.59 × 7 = $4.13
ALTERNATE: $.59 × 3 = $1.77 (food for 3 cats for 1 day); $1.77 × 7 = $12.39 (food for 3 cats for 1 week)

3. 2 × 5 fruit chews a week = 10 fruit chews a week
$.39 × 10 = $3.90

4. 6 × $2.00 = $12.00
$12.00 ÷ $.75 = 16; she has enough for 16 fish.

5. Assuming 4 weeks in a month: 4 × 4 batteries = 16 batteries
Must buy 3 packs of 6 to get 16 (2 will be left over).
3 × $4.10 = $12.30

6. $.80 × $.06 = $.048 or $.05; $.80 + $.05 = $.85 (cost for 2 packages with tax)
$10 ÷ $.85 = 11.76 2-pack sets (cannot buy fraction of a 2-pack set, so she can buy 11)
11 × 2 = 22 packages

Set 15 (pages 40–41)

1. Cheddar per pound = $1 ($4.00 ÷ 4 pounds)
   String per pound = $1.40 ($2.80 ÷ 2 pounds)
   Swiss per pound = $1.20 ($3.60 ÷ 3 pounds)
   Cheddar is the best buy.

2. $1.69 ÷ 2 = $.85 per battery; $3.29 ÷ 4 = $.82 per battery
   $4.75 ÷ 6 = $.79 per battery; $5.99 ÷ 8 = $.75 per battery
   The 8-pack is the best buy.

3. $.99 ÷ 50 = $.02 per foot for gold ribbon
   $3.00 ÷ 100 = $.03 per foot for red cord
   $1.20 ÷ 80 = $.015 per foot for green ribbon
   Green ribbon is the best buy.

4. Chocolate drops: $2.50 ÷ 16 = $.16 per ounce
   Mint chews: $3.00 ÷ 48 (or $1.50 ÷ 24) = $.06 per ounce
   Caramels: $1.50 ÷ 14 = $.11 per ounce
   Mint chews are the best buy.

5. Butter cookies: $2.99 ÷ 32 = $.09 per ounce
   Sandwich cookies: $4.99 ÷ 36 = $.14 per ounce
   Butter cookies are the better buy.

6. Sweet potatoes: $.89 ÷ 2 = $.45 per pound (rounded up)
   White potatoes: $1.29 ÷ 3 = $.43 per pound
   Yellow potatoes are $.49 per pound
   White potatoes are the best buy.

Set 16 (pages 42–43)

1. 3,900 − 1,552 = 2,348 miles

2. 50 yards × 3 = 150 feet (width of soccer field)
   160 feet is more than 150 feet, so the football field is wider.
   ALTERNATE: football field: 360 feet × 160 feet = 57,600 square feet
   soccer field: 300 feet × 150 feet = 45,000 square feet
   The football field has greater area.

3. 20 + 7 = 27 feet wide
   40 feet + 38 feet = 78 feet
   27 feet by 78 feet

4. Jefferson School: 230 × 120 = 27,600 square feet
   Adams School: 220 × 130 = 28,600 square feet
   Adams School's playground has the larger area.

5. 2,390 + 58 = 2,448 miles

6. 19,850 + 470 = 20,320 feet

Set 17 (pages 44–45)

1. 1,900 + 1,700 + 1,400 + 1,300 = 6,300 feet climbed
   7,574 − 6,300 = 1,274 feet left

2. 371 + 432 + 393 = 1,196 miles
   1,560 − 1,196 = 364 miles

3. 2,000 + 1,286 + 1,400 = 4,686 miles
   4,686 ÷ 300 = 15.62 days or 16 days

4. 42 + 48 + 36 + 47 = 173 miles
   200 − 173 = 27 miles

5. 2 + 3 = 5 miles (one way); 2 × 5 = 10 miles (round-trip)
   5 days × 10 miles = 50 miles

6. 1 + 1 = 2 miles each day round trip
   9 × 2 = 18 miles

Set 18 (pages 46–47)

1. 15 minutes to mix
   5 minutes × 6 batches = 30 minutes to get cookies ready
   15 minutes × 6 batches = 90 minutes to bake
   15 + 30 + 90 = 135 minutes or 2 hours 15 minutes
   2:00 P.M. + 2 hours 15 minutes = 4:15 P.M.

2. 10:15 A.M. + 10 minutes + 15 minutes = 10:40 A.M. arrive at subway station
   10:40 A.M. + 3 minutes + 20 minutes = 11:03 A.M. arrive at streetcar stop
   11:03 A.M. + 6 + 15 = 11:24 A.M. arrive at library
   Yes, he's on time.

3. 9:30 A.M. + 35 minutes = 10:05 A.M.; 10:05 A.M. + 2 hours = 12:05 P.M.
   12:05 P.M. + 20 minutes = 12:25 P.M.; 12:25 P.M.+ 1 hour = 1:25 P.M.

4. 4:15 P.M. − 1 hour = 3:15 P.M.; 3:15 P.M. − 30 minutes = 2:45 P.M.
   2:45 P.M. − 20 minutes = 2:25 P.M.; 2:25 P.M. − 4 hours = 10:25 A.M.
   10:25 A.M. − 10 minutes = 10:15 A.M.; 10:15 A.M. − 10 minutes = 10:05 A.M.

5. 6:00 P.M. − 5 hours = 1:00 P.M.; 1:00 P.M. − 30 minutes = 12:30 P.M.
   12:30 P.M. − 45 minutes = 11:45 A.M.; 11:45 A.M. − 20 minutes = 11:25 A.M

6. 9:30 A.M. + 15 minutes = 9:45 A.M.; 9:45 A.M. + 25 minutes = 10:10 A.M.; 10:10 A.M. + 1 hour = 11:10 A.M.; 11:10 A.M. + 25 minutes = 11:35 A.M.

Set 19 (pages 48–49)

1. 290 miles ÷ 50 miles per hour = 5.8 hours
   ALTERNATE: .10 of an hour = 6 minutes; 6 minutes × 8 = 48, so trip will take 5 hours and 48 minutes.

2. Family can take 8 days for driving (4 out and 4 back).
   1,676 miles ÷ 4 days = 419 miles each day, each way

3. 2,680 miles ÷ 600 miles per hour = 4.47 hours for the flight (or about $4\frac{1}{2}$ hours)

4. 1,572 miles ÷ 3 days = 524 miles

5. 2,629 miles ÷ 400 miles per day = 6.57 days (about $6\frac{1}{2}$ days)

6. 720 miles ÷ 360 miles = 2 days (one way) x 2 = 4 days (round-trip)

Set 20 (pages 50–51)

1. Two walls are 12 x 8 = 96 square feet (each)
Two walls are 24 x 8 = 192 square feet (each)
96 + 96 + 192 + 192 = 576 square feet total
576 ÷ 10 (square foot coverage of one quart) = 57.6 quarts
Must buy 58 quarts (must round up from 57.6; can't purchase fraction of container).
ALTERNATE: 58 quarts ÷ 4 quarts = 14.5 gallons, so must round up and buy 15 gallons.

2. 10 x 13 = 130 square feet; 9 x 12 = 108 square feet; 5 x 3 = 15 square feet
130 + 108 + 15 = 253 square feet
ALTERNATE: 253 ÷ 9 = 28 square yards

3. 36 + 36 = 72 feet to be strung with balloons
12 ÷ 4 = 3 balloons per foot
3 x 72 = 216 balloons

4. 25 x 2 = 50 feet (two walls); 50 x 2 = 100 feet (two walls); 150 feet total
150 ÷ 10 = 15 packages
ALTERNATE: 15 x $4.95 = $74.25

5. 10 x 12 inches = 120 inches; 120 ÷ 6 = 20
On the first 10-foot edge, she'll plant 20 plants.
20 x 12 = 240; 240 ÷ 6 = 40
On the first 20-foot edge, she'll plant 39 (the one in the corner of the first edge is shared).
On the next 10-foot edge, she'll plant 19 (the one in the corner of the second edge is shared).
On the last 20-foot edge, she'll plant 38 (the two corners are already covered).
20 + 39 + 19 + 38 = 116 plants needed; 116 ÷ 6 flats = 19 flats with a remainder of 1. She will have to buy 20 flats to get the 116 plants she needs.

6. He can fit 6 posters along the length of the wall (144 inches ÷ 24 inches= 6).
He can fit 3 posters on the height (108 inches ÷ 36 inches = 3).
6 x 3 = 18 posters will cover the wall.

Set 21 (pages 52–53)

1. 12 x 2 = 24 (length, which is twice as long as width)
12 + 12 + 24 + 24 = 72-foot perimeter
ALTERNATE: 24 x 12 = 288 square feet

2. 10 x 26 = 260 square feet; 20 x 30 = 600 square feet
260 + 600 = 860 square feet total area

3. 45 + 45 = 90; 60 + 60 = 120; 90 + 120 = 210 feet
210 – 12 (width of 2 doors) = 198 feet

4. 12 x 15 = 180 square feet (area of one wall)
180 x 2 = 360 square feet (total area of both walls)

5. Front area: 120 + 120 + 300 = 540 feet of fencing
Back area: 180 + 180 + 300 = 660 feet of fencing
540 + 660 = 1,200 feet of fencing

6. 12 x 12 = 144 square feet; 6 x 20 = 120 square feet; 8 x 12 = 96 square feet
144 + 120 + 96 = 360 square feet

FRACTIONS AND PERCENTS

Set 22 (pages 54–55)

1. There is more carrot cake left over because $\frac{1}{3}$ is more than $\frac{1}{4}$.
ALTERNATE: $\frac{1}{4}$ of 24 = 6 pieces of chocolate cake left over; $\frac{1}{3}$ of 24 = 8 pieces of carrot cake left over.

2. $\frac{1}{2}$ of $\frac{1}{2}$ is the same as $\frac{2}{8}$; both equal $\frac{1}{4}$.

3. The blue strips are the widest because $\frac{5}{8}$ is wider than $\frac{1}{2}$ or $\frac{1}{3}$.
ALTERNATE: $\frac{5}{8} = \frac{15}{24}$; $\frac{1}{2} = \frac{14}{24}$; $\frac{1}{3} = \frac{8}{24}$. $\frac{15}{24} + \frac{12}{24} + \frac{8}{24} = \frac{35}{24}$ or $1\frac{11}{24}$

4. $\frac{2}{8}$ of a pound is $\frac{1}{4}$ of a pound. Since there are 4 children, this is the amount that each child should get. ($\frac{2}{6} = \frac{1}{3}$, and neither that nor $\frac{1}{5}$ can be given to each of the 4 children.)

5. Amos should choose package number 3. ($\frac{4}{5}$ is greater than $\frac{1}{2}$ of a pound or $\frac{3}{8}$ of a pound.)

6. Pizza got the most votes because $\frac{2}{5}$ is greater than $\frac{1}{6}$, $\frac{1}{3}$, or $\frac{1}{10}$.
ALTERNATE: Pizza got 12 votes; tacos got 5 votes; spaghetti got 10 votes; and grilled cheese got 3 votes.

Set 23 (pages 56–57)

1. There are two ways:
(1) $\frac{1}{8} + \frac{3}{8} + \frac{1}{2}$
(2) $\frac{1}{8} + \frac{1}{8}$ (using the same color) $+ \frac{1}{4} + \frac{1}{2}$

2. He can make two 2-inch lengths by first combining two 1-inch pieces, then combining the $1\frac{1}{2}$-inch piece with the $\frac{1}{2}$-inch piece.

3. There are two ways of making an 8-inch strip:
(1) Put a yellow piece and a blue piece together.
(2) Put 3 red strips and a yellow strip together.

4. There are 3 obvious ways: 2 cups of graham flour; $\frac{1}{2}$ cup barley flour and $1\frac{1}{2}$ cup rye flour; $\frac{1}{4}$ cup oat flour, $\frac{3}{4}$ cup wheat flour, and 1 cup graham flour.
Or use partial amounts, e.g.: $\frac{1}{4}$ cup barley flour, $\frac{1}{4}$ cup oat flour, $1\frac{1}{2}$ cups rye flour.

5. The most obvious combinations are:
   (a) $\frac{1}{2}$ cup pintos, $\frac{1}{2}$ cup limas, $\frac{3}{4}$ cup navy, and $\frac{1}{4}$ cup black beans;
   (b) $1\frac{1}{2}$ cups garbanzos and $\frac{1}{2}$ cup pintos; (c) $1\frac{1}{2}$ cups garbanzos and $\frac{1}{2}$ cup limas.
   Or use partial amounts, e.g., $\frac{1}{2}$ cup each of four different kinds.

6. Each bowl should have $1\frac{1}{4}$ cups jelly beans, $\frac{3}{4}$ cup of gumdrops, and $\frac{1}{2}$ cup of peppermints.

Set 24 (pages 58–59)

1. $\frac{1}{2} + \frac{1}{4} + \frac{1}{8} = \frac{7}{8}$ pound
2. $1\frac{1}{2} + \frac{3}{4} + 2 = 4\frac{1}{4}$ pounds
   ALTERNATE: At $1 a pound, the fruit cost $4.25 all together.
3. $\frac{1}{4} + \frac{1}{2} + \frac{3}{4} = 1\frac{1}{2}$ pounds
4. $\frac{2}{3}$ (pinto) + $\frac{1}{4}$ (kidney) + $\frac{1}{3}$ (black) = $1\frac{1}{4}$ pounds
   ALTERNATE: $\frac{2}{3}$ of $.60 = $.40; $\frac{1}{4}$ of $.80 = $.20; $\frac{1}{3}$ of $.90 = $.30; $.40 + $.20 + $.30 = $.90
5. $2\frac{1}{2}$ cups wheat + $\frac{1}{2}$ cup oat = 3 cups
   $\frac{3}{4}$ cup barley + $\frac{1}{4}$ cup rye = 1 cup
   3 cups + 1 cup = 4 cups all together
6. 2 cups walnuts + $\frac{3}{4}$ cup almonds + $1\frac{1}{2}$ cups pecans = $4\frac{1}{4}$ cups nuts
   1 cup dates + $\frac{3}{4}$ cup figs + $\frac{1}{2}$ cup apricots = $2\frac{1}{4}$ cups fruit
   $4\frac{1}{4} + 2\frac{1}{4} = 6\frac{1}{2}$ cups fruit-nut mix

Set 25 (pages 60–61)

1. $12 \div 2 = 6$ pieces left over; $6 \times 2 = 12$ pieces left over from 2 pizzas
   $12 \div 3 = 4$ pieces left over; $4 \times 2 = 8$ pieces left over from 2 pizzas
   $12 + 8 = 20$ pieces left over in all
2. $\frac{1}{2}$ of 1 pie = 3 pieces; $3 \times 2 = 6$ pieces
   $\frac{1}{3}$ of 1 pie = 2 pieces; $2 \times 2 = 4$ pieces
   $6 + 4 = 10$ pieces
3. $24 \div 4 = 6$ ($\frac{1}{4}$ of one pan); $6 \times 3 = 18$ (chocolate pieces left over)
   $24 \div 3 = 8$ ($\frac{1}{3}$ of one pan); $2 \times 8 = 16$ (vanilla pieces left over)
   $18 + 16 = 34$ pieces
4. 6 (cans) × 6 (packs) × 6 (cases) = 216 cans to start
   $216 \div 4 = 54$ cans consumed; $216 - 54 = 162$ cans
5. $\frac{1}{2}$ of 10 = 5 eaten (5 left); $5 \times 2 = 10$ left
   $\frac{2}{5}$ of 10 = 4 eaten (6 left); $6 \times 2 = 12$ left
   $\frac{1}{5}$ of 10 = 2 eaten (8 left)
   $10 + 12 + 8 = 30$

6. 12 ate 2 each (12 × 2 = 24)
   6 ate 3 each (6 × 3 = 18); 6 ate 4 each (6 × 4 = 24)
   24 + 18 + 24 = 66 cookies eaten
   6 × 12 = 72 cookies to start; 72 − 66 = 6 cookies

Set 26 (pages 62–63)

1. Less than one hour = 25%; 1–2 hours = 50%; 2–3 hours = 12.5%; more than 3 hours = 12.5%
2. There were 25 of each kind of cookie, so $\frac{1}{5}$ of each kind = 5.
   Eaten: 35 total (10 oatmeal, 5 peanut butter, 5 lemon, and 15 walnut)
   $100 - 35 = 65$ of 100 cookies left over, or 65%
3. $\frac{3}{8} + \frac{3}{8} = \frac{6}{8}$ or $\frac{3}{4}$ have views of downtown.
   $\frac{3}{4} = 75\%$
4. 19% + 21% + 20% + 15% = 75%
   75% = $\frac{3}{4}$ of the student body
5. Since toffee and peppermint made up 60% of the mix, licorice and butterscotch, being in equal parts, made up 20% each.
   20% = $\frac{1}{5}$, so butterscotch was $\frac{1}{5}$ of the mix
   ALTERNATE: $\frac{1}{5}$ of 200 = 40 pieces of butterscotch
6. Soccer: 16 of 32 = $\frac{1}{2}$ = 50%
   Softball: 12 of 32 = $\frac{3}{8}$ = 37.5%
   Tennis: 4 of 32 = $\frac{1}{8}$ = 12.5%

RATES, AVERAGES, AND LOGICAL REASONING

Set 27 (pages 64–65)

1. Each number in the sequence is double the preceding number (8, 16, 32), so the next number is 64.
2. Each number in the sequence is 4 less than the preceding number (21, 17, 13), so the rat will eat 5 pellets on the fifth day.
3. Louis checks books out every 7 days, and each number of books is 3 more than the preceding number (15, 18, 21), so the next number, for March 22, is 24, and the number for March 29 is 27.
4. Each number in the sequence is three times the preceding number (2, 6, 18). The next two numbers are 54 and 162; 54 fish for Raul's thirteenth birthday and 162 for his fourteenth.
5. Each number in the sequence is 12 more than the preceding number (42, 54, 66, 78), so the next three numbers are 90, 102, 114.
   She will hit 114 balls on the seventh Saturday.
6. Each number in the sequence is 21 less than the preceding number (403, 382, 361), so the next four

numbers are 340, 319, 298, 277. The theater will sell 277 tickets the next Friday night.

Set 28 (pages 66–67)

1. 3 boxes per minute × 45 minutes = 135 boxes (more than needed)
Yes, Mike can fold 100 boxes by 6 P.M.

2. Every 2 minutes, she can make 4 sandwiches, so it will take her 50 minutes to make 100 and 200 minutes to make 400.
200 minutes = 3 hours 20 minutes, so she must start at 8:40 A.M.

3. At 1.5 minutes per lap, it will take him 75 minutes to swim 50 laps (1.5 × 50 = 75)
ALTERNATE: Starting at 9 A.M., he will finish at 10:15 A.M.

4. At 4 pretzels a minute, it takes them 3 minutes to form 1 dozen.
3 minutes × 6 dozen = 18 minutes

5. They wash 8 cars an hour (each team washes one car every 15 minutes).
In 3 hours, they wash 24 cars.

6. At 400 a minute, the machine makes 24,000 an hour (400 × 60).
ALTERNATE: 24,000 × 7 hours = 168,000 a day

Set 29 (pages 68–69)

1. 99 + 87 + 115 + 107 = 408 total harvest
408 ÷ 4 = 102 is the average number harvested per person

2. 67 + 68 + 74 + 77 + 69 + 65 + 63 = 483
483 ÷ 7 = 69 was the average temperature

3. 49 + 53 + 57 + 55 + 46 = 260
260 ÷ 5 = 52 was the average number of people on the bus each day

4. 12 + 12 + 14 + 14 + 10 + 13 + 16 = 91
91 ÷ 7 = 13 ounces was the average weight of the kittens

5. 408 + 416 + 420 + 420 + 411 = 2,075
2,075 ÷ 5 = 415 is the average daily attendance

6. After converting heights to inches: (57 × 5) + (59 × 4) + (60 × 3) + (62 × 3) + (64 × 2) + 65 = 285 + 236 + 180 + 186 + 128 + 65 = 1,080
1,080 ÷ 18 = 60 inches (5 feet) is the average height

Set 30 (pages 70–71)

1. At Franklin, 10 maples planted
At McClure, 6 oaks planted + 2 maples from truck
12 maples + 6 oaks = 18 trees were in the truck at the start

2. 10 − 6 = 4 rides left on first ticket
10 − 5 = 5 rides left on second ticket
10 − 1 = 9 rides left on third ticket
4 + 5 + 9 = 18 rides left

3. Second Saturday: 3 books kept + 7 new books = 10 books
Monday: 10 − 2 = 8 books kept + 1 new book = 9 books in all

4. On Friday, the boys are even, so Julius doesn't owe Ira anything.

5. Donated 40; purchased 16.
Donated 20; purchased 23.
20 (never donated) + 16 + 23 = 59 books

6. 2 × 2 = 4 apples given to friends + 1 to Officer Smith
3 lost in street + 2 to the lady next door
4 + 1 + 3 + 2 = 10; 10 + 13 = 23 apples bought at market

Appendix: Predicting the Question

As students read each part of a think-aloud word problem, they will make predictions about what the final question will be. (As an extension activity, you might choose to have students answer some of the questions they come up with.) The examples below illustrate ways of generating possible questions. If students are having difficulty predicting the question, you may want to model the process by walking them through these questions.

Set 1, Problem 1

PART 1: The Initial Premise

Joe likes to collect and trade watches. On Friday, he had 23 watches in his collection.

* Joe might get a job to earn money to buy more watches. The question might ask how many hours he has to work to earn money for one more watch. If that's the question, we'll need to know how much one watch costs and how much money he can earn in an hour. Then we'd have to divide the cost of a watch by the amount of money he can earn in an hour to see how many hours he will have to work to buy another watch.

* Joe might trade some of his watches for better ones. In that case, the question might ask how many he ends up with after several trades. If that's the question, we'll need to know how many he gives and how many he receives. We'd have to subtract and add to get the answer.

PART 2: Additional Information

On Saturday, he went to a flea market and bought 4 more watches for $2.00 each. On Sunday, he went to 3 garage sales and bought 2 watches at each sale for $1.00 each.

* The question might ask how much he spent altogether at the flea market or at the two garage sales together. If that's the question, we don't need any more information. To get the answer, we'd have to multiply and add.

* Or the question might ask how many more watches Joe needs if he wants to have 50 in his collection. If that's the question, we don't need any more information. To get the answer, we'd have to add and subtract.

PART 3: The Question

How many watches did Joe have on Sunday after his last purchase?

* Answer: 23 watches + 4 more on Saturday = 27
  $27 + (2 \times 3) = 33$ watches

Set 6, Problem 6

Part 1: The Initial Premise

Takisha's mother got a new cell phone with a plan that allows 400 minutes of calls each month for $15.95. The plan charges extra if she uses more than 400 minutes. She asks Takisha to keep track of the minutes she uses.

* The question might ask the average number of minutes Takisha's mother uses each day. If that's the question, we'd have to know the number of days in a month. Then we'd have to divide 400 by that number. If that's the question, then the information about costs and excess time aren't relevant.

* Or the question might ask how much Takisha's mother will spend in a year for the phone, if she always stays within the 400-minute limit. We know there are 12 months in a year, so we don't need any more information. We'd have to multiply $15.95 by 12 to get the answer.

PART 2: Additional Information

In the first week, she used 15 minutes each day for 5 days, and in the second week she used 25 minutes a day for 4 days. In the third week she used 32 minutes each day for 4 days, and in the fourth week, she used 20 minutes a day for 4 days.

* The question might ask in which week Takisha's mother spent the longest amount of time on the phone. We don't need any more information to figure that out. To get the answer, we'd have to multiply the daily amount by the number of days for each week and then see which week had the highest number.

* Or the question might ask how much more time the mother used in one week, compared to another week. If that's the question, we don't need more information. To get the answer, we'd have to multiply minutes by days for each week, then subtract to get the difference.

PART 3: The Question

Did Takisha's mother stay within the 400-minute limit?

* Answer: $(15 \times 5) + (25 \times 4) = 175$ minutes for weeks 1 and 2
  $(32 \times 4) + (20 \times 4) = 208$ minutes for weeks 3 and 4
  $175 + 208 = 383$; Takisha's mother stayed within her limit.